The Dimensions
of Companionship

The Dimensions of Companionship

An Assessment of Modern Emotional and Material Needs in Relation to Marriage

Paul Dennis Sporer

QUENSTEDT PRESS

ANZA PUBLISHING, Chester, New York
Quenstedt Press is an imprint of Anza Publishing
Copyright © 2010 by Paul Dennis Sporer

Library of Congress Cataloguing-in-Publication Data
Sporer, Paul D.
    The dimensions of companionship /
    Paul Dennis Sporer.
        p. cm.
    Includes bibliographical references and index.
    ISBN-13: 978–1–932490–34–3 (softcover : alk. paper)
    ISBN-10: 1–932490–34–5 (softcover : alk. paper)
    1. Family. 2. Parent and child. I. Title.
    HQ519.S66 2008
    306.81—dc22   2008044640

Visit AnzaPublishing.com for more information on
outstanding authors and titles. Please support our efforts
to restore great literature to a place of prominence in
our culture.

ISBN-13: 978–1–932490–34–3 (softcover)

⊗ This book is printed on acid-free paper.

To my dearest Cassandra

CONTENTS

Chapter 1

Introduction

 $\mathcal{T}$ here are in the minds of young children, certain powerful archetypes that urge fulfilment as pellucid concepts; even if they do not have an expansive understanding of these archetypes, they can turn them into a constellation of mental activity using their imagination. Children can place on a mental stage actors and actresses who express these concepts, through their personalities, habits, goals, and desires. Thus, the sublime takes shape and substance. In this deeper view of life, magnificent and majestic conceptual areas are now emerging into consciousness: Patronage, Education, Occupation, Emotional Satisfaction, Finances, and Community. As children become adults, these Fundamentals take on even greater force and relevance. Indeed, these areas, each forceful and complex in itself, echoes and re-echoes throughout the vast social spaces in the history in the Western world. More than just needs, they are edifices, that stand on their own. However, when integrated, they engender solid, enduring attitudes towards the healthy development of intellect and reason, and they spur life-enhancing activity that can fulfill cherished dreams and ambitions. Therefore, everyone seeks out in which domain are the lines are drawn that interconnect these edifices. From their observations of their parents, even young children are aware, on some level, that family life presents a confluence of the great Fundamentals.

Hence, the mix of issues in married life can be divided into two broad categories, *the material and the psychological*. It is self-evident that material issues are not the only considerations in the decision to marry, as psychological factors must figure in as well. However, even though people openly dealt, with great seriousness, the changing economic circumstances that they observed, they only indirectly addressed the individualistic issues of personality and temperament. This is not to say that they ignored these personal factors; indeed, they gave them substantial weight in their life 'equation'. But personal factors, as topics of conversations, were introduced and examined with delicacy and tact, and were not as candidly discussed as were the issues of money, work, possessions or taxes.

Although the material and psychological areas can be effectively separated—such as for political debate, social study, or media attention—these two areas often merge in an almost esoteric manner. One area affects the other, cross influences are present that are difficult to discern, and even more difficult to stop. Indeed, it is in the family of childhood that perhaps we can best observe this mystical union of the material and psychological in relation to intimate, companionate relationships.

One might ask: How have people throughout the course of civilisation, interrelated psychological and emotional demands, with economic and material conditions? Let us consider this question, and then we can turn to studying the specific types of psychological requirements, within the context of a modern society governed by an independence-orientated mentality.

Firstly, we should understand that unlike material factors, many mental aspects of human nature do not change very much over time. Basic needs do not change, but the manner in which they are satisfied is subject to alteration. Even though a particular idea as to how to satisfy one of the above Fundamentals might be perceived as 'modern', the desire itself might nevertheless be of ancient origin. But short of using a time machine, we have no way of knowing with any great certainty how the general public looked at these issues in remote times. Today, we have far more information about individual attitudes, which gives us knowledge about the dynamics that influence people to marry. But, in the Western world, this detailed information is extant only the late 1800s. It is logical to assume that, if there is a period of time where the dynamics have not changed in three to five generations, for example from the late 1800s to the mid-1900s, then they are part of a longer trend, probably much longer. In regard to the manner in which people deal with the primary issues related to marriage, we can safely apply certain principles found in the 'modern' period in the Western nations, within reason, to the cultures of the more distant past, from whom we are ultimately descended, not only physically but culturally and morally. This historical depth should lead us to appreciate the singularity, the unusual nature, of a very recent metamorphosis in attitudes concerning companionship.

Drawing upon our own personal understanding of the universal need for 'fulfilment', that is, attaining all that one desires but lacks, we discover this need to be an unchanging, absolutely constant factor in human nature. Throughout the many centuries before the modern age, when life was otherwise tedious, bleak and threatening, one kept hope alive that one would eventually see the consummation of the material, intellectual and emotional; indeed, this prospect kept one from sliding into pessimism and cynicism.

We can say confidently, that the most important aspect of the male-female relationship that has not been abandoned is the ideal of *total mutual affection*, since maximum contentment is gotten through an all-encompassing love with a person of the opposite sex. Indeed, in some men the ideal burns strongly. As in the past, these men may remain single past the average marriage age, because they have formed an ideal of the feminine in adolescence, but they never find the woman that fits this ideal, and so prefer to stay single rather than marry someone who does not meet their high standards.[1] There is nothing inherently wrong with this, and oftentimes, such a man was praised as being virtuous due to the uncompromising nature of his character in such important areas. Preserving the ideal of affection becomes central to one's identity and existence, more so than gaining partial emotional fulfilment. Of course, men and women who marry at the average age or at an early age might have ideals as well, but they are not as lofty as the late or never-marrying.

Finding failure with ordinary women, the idealist draws energy from his concept of femininity, which exists as the imagination's 'perfect woman'. The ideal woman responds, as an antipode, to all the imperfect behaviour in the world, and a real wife would necessarily displace this Venus. Thus, people who marry late or never may have less interest in 'ordinary' marriage, precisely because they have very *high* standards. A fairly permanent standard is erected early in life, and efforts to dismantle it can lead to resistance, if not hostility. Most men, however, who ardently value these precepts formed in childhood will be sadly disappointed by the inability to make the ideal come to life. Individuals with high ideals about the role of love in marriage, but who achieve little in the way of bringing about this standard, are clearly more interested in retaining the ideal, rather than enjoying the benefits of marriage, although both areas are meaningful to them. Thinking of this kind often throws a spanner into the works of sociology, since it is not based on 'rational' considerations, easily measured factors such as income, status, education, but instead on soft 'irrational' notions. Yet, that this is an important facet of male-female relationships cannot be denied.

In the healthy idealistic scenario, the individual seeks the person, the romantic and virtuous 'beloved', *who would balance out their own weaknesses, both material and emotional, leading to psychological wholeness.* The psychological satisfaction derived from a passionate, romantic attachment between a man and women could be fulfilled by establishing an equilibrium, when both persons are ready to make sacrifices for the deepening the relationship. In this way is the ideal truly brought to life. Hence, *complementarity,* the dovetailing of differences between people, has always been a critical factor in reaching the ideal of love. Yet, as time has gone on, the uncompromising nature has become more difficult to maintain, and concessions to 'realism' had to be made. In the 20th century, it became difficult to achieve this mutually enhancing differences in experiences and temperament. This was caused by more self-centeredness, greater intolerance of personality differences, and less necessity for complementarity due to changes in household function. Determining and handling similarity is easier than managing the complexities of dissimilarity, and so when similarity became the focus of the search for a marriage partner, the belief developed that a love match could be easily made. Naturally, dealing with personality and background differences are still as important as ever, but discussions about such issues have become sparse. Less time and effort were invested in ascertaining a person's acceptability as marriage partner. In addition, the 'popularisation' of the analytical, and increasing education of the population, an outgrowth of the same forces that created the possibility of more similitude in marriage (as duties were transferred from mother and father to companies and schools), rendered a certain foreignness to deep positive emotion. This, combined with shorter courtship period, led to many poor choices of marriage partners, with resulting problematic divorce rates. The necessity of maximising the interrelationship between human similarities and differences in reaching personal fulfilment is an important area of study, especially within the context of historical developments (for in-depth discussions about these issues, see Sporer 2010B).

We can legitimately conclude that men and women are still *captivated by the ideal,* and they seek to reach it, but due to particular, and peculiar, issues of modern existence, they fail. Perhaps this partially explains the paradox why the people of the current time, who supposedly strongly believe in a *romantic* notion of marriage, are often unwilling to make the sacrifices necessary to achieve stable relationships; they are unwilling to marry early, and indeed often unwilling to marry at all. They wish to preserve this poorly conceived ideal, and so they seek, perhaps as in past times, the companion they imagine, but now the long road does not lead to triumph, but only to a sad comprehension about the contradictions and hypocrisies present in many relationships. From observations of modern life, key questions arise that revolve around the issues of autonomy and love. How can one proclaim to be looking for a Mr Right or Miss Right, but yet marry someone that was clearly never 'right' to begin with? How can one be both consciously seeking that single 'true love', but yet have numerous sex partners? How can couples advocate marriage as the only place where the warmth of true companionship can occur, yet doggedly pursue a career, when it even threatens to dismiss love and affection?

In light of these competing factors and disappointments, it might be thought that the importance of marriage is dwindling, with a parallel rise in the *satisfaction of being unmarried*. In fact, this is *not* the case. More than ever, people want to marry, although they may not be fully conscious of this desire. We find that the differences in well-being between married and unmarried are *increasing*, not decreasing. Differences in happiness appear greatest in the most *modern* European cultures, whereas almost none exist in the traditional ones. Married persons are becoming more dependent on spouses, not less; overall happiness in life has become intimately tied with satisfaction in marriage. Not surprisingly, between 1950 and 1980 suicide rates rose far more for the unmarried than the married.[2] All of this points to the increasing isolation of marriage as providing gratification to the *exclusion* of other relationships and institutions, a critical fact we should not ignore.

The truth is that it is still possible to obtain satisfaction with ordinary friendships, yet overcoming the superficial aspects of non-marital relationships is becoming increasingly difficult. In the past, when people could get emotional satisfaction from a job, hobby, or close relationships with a small circle of relatives and friends, there was no significant correlation between the number of one's friends and marital tendency. Today, *quantity* of friendship is a key factor, more so than quality, and it is thought, albeit incorrectly, that a social situation containing many 'friends' can substitute for marriage and bring fulfilment. Perhaps if one has many more than the average number of friends, one can permanently delay marriage. However, in the past, in the absence of friends, people might *not* have married more quickly. Why have people obtained relatively little emotional fulfilment from non-marital relationships in our day, and why have people, paradoxically, become more dependent on such relationships? The reasons are varied: Relationships are less stable and less homogeneous, due to people coming from more diverse backgrounds and different geographical areas; there is a preoccupation with materialism, instead of character, intellect and spirituality; diversions in the form of mass entertainment make it less necessary to cultivate friendships.

Thus, many people become dissatisfied with their friendships, and desire a deeper, long-lasting, intimate relationship, that has clear boundaries and obligations. We can say that, anytime there is a great desire for something, *without a viable plan*, an unsafe situation is created. The male-female intimate friendship is ostensibly critical to one's success in life, but many paradoxically spend little time working to achieve such a relationship. Moreover, in spite of attaining some security in one's life, the average individual too often relies on one person, who clearly does not bring the emotional satisfaction that is wanted. It is irrefutable that such a 'partner' was chosen rashly and heedlessly, the result of a quick pragmatic search, but where older traditional courtship principles were ignored. In a specific, and fairly rigidly defined, cultural context such as marriage, the contemporary 'match' often brings not peace but friction, especially when the relationship itself is based on physical factors, not spiritual or psychological ones. The streets of modern life are filled with often troubled and struggling characters, not the joyous, secure people envisioned by our parents and grandparents. The yearning for love is still so great, yet the men and women who try to satisfy this yearning often end up dejected and lonely.

As relationship ideals are intensely personal, only the individual can bear the ultimate responsibility in choosing the correct method to reach these ideals. However, assistance in the construction of plans and methods should always be welcome. In this regard, *traditions* have laid out clear paths that will assist the individual in attaining psychological wholeness and fulfilment. What is important to note, is that these *traditional principles always clearly consider both the psychological and material aspects to relationships*; they are not simply idle 'pie in the sky' musings, nor are they cold, authoritarian dictates.

Traditional society understood that the ideal of love is not realised by merely 'reaching a place', but is found in continuing success in jointly overcoming material obstacles in life, and in enjoying life's most profound spiritual, intellectual, and artistic offerings. The recommended actions along the path prepare the individual financially, mentally and emotionally. Some might worry, however, that too much freedom might be lost by following this course, freedom which could be used to develop schooling, career and personality. Nonetheless, there does not appear to be any recurring conflict between educational experiences, educational attainment and acting out the positive traditional role in the family.[3] Each step in the process, when taken with deliberation and accepted on its own terms, does not necessarily negatively affect any other step.

The modern Western world has retained certain aspects of the traditional; the usual or typical route is for a man or woman to finish their education, then begin a full-time career, then marry, then have children. After this point, the sexes have somewhat different paths: Women often must leave work for a period of time, and then possibly return to full-time or part-time labour force participation. After the children have grown up and left home, the parents have an admittedly ambiguous role. The path, as presented here, does not merely end with the wedding, and the couple live 'happily ever after', but involves activities that are antecedent to marriage, and activities that carry on well beyond the maturation of the youngest child in the family.

There are, of course, restrictions in the life path that create discernible patterns of behaviour. These restrictions are often material in nature, and can be overcome using an intelligent, logical plan. For example, women who marry late tend to be individuals who are in the process of acquiring higher education or pursuing careers, and, not surprisingly, are often of conservative background, through which traditional segmentation between roles can be transmitted. In the United States, these women often tend to be middle-class Roman Catholics, who marry outside of their class and work only until the first birth. Such a pattern is indicative of individuals who plan carefully by amassing greater economic resources.[4] Those with traditional conceptions about family life, such as devout Catholics, understand the need to *settle* into a role, before moving on to the next stage. They first put aside marriage plans to concentrate on obtaining an education, and then establishing themselves in a well-paying job. They then save money so as to establish themselves again, this time in the domestic role, which allows them to remain at home with their children. The weak link in the chain might be the personality of the marriage partner, who might have been chosen hastily.[5]

Hence, interrelating the wise precepts of European tradition with the complex demands of the modern age is difficult. However, there are situations where the various strands of ideals, education, career and materialism—using both traditional and modern materials—have been most *successfully* woven together. Let us take the example of Madrid, Spain.[6] Even in the 1980s, this area was a fairly typical example of a contemporary Catholic and traditional, though urban, culture. For young people, dating begins at about age 16, serious dating by age 18, with the ideal marriage age being 23. There is fairly good agreement between theory and practise, with one-third marrying within one year of the marriage age ideal, and if outside of this range, the tendency is to marry later than the ideal age. Individuals have a relatively free hand in choosing a mate; indeed, many parents do not even know the person their son or daughter is seeing. Although persistent reinforcement of independence ideals, as would are found in more modern countries, is absent, the desire for *self-sufficiency* is nevertheless strong, and relatively few couples receive money from parents (25%) or share an apartment with their parents after marriage (33%). However, they maintain that economic considerations are not generally important in affecting the disposition to marry (37% say they are), but they are more important in affecting the length of courtship.

Couples desire to live in a well-furnished residence separate from the parental abodes, an arrangement which necessitates careful accumulation of domestic items and furniture whilst putting money aside. Hence, the period of steady dating and engagement is by Western European standards quite long, usually lasting nearly four years, with even longer courtships being acceptable. Specific economic factors which force sons or daughters to leave home, in order to work might create unusually long courtships. They marry *later* because they give most of their income over to their families, without being able to save much for themselves. Leaving home to work is more a case of economic necessity to support the family, rather than fulfilling a desire to be autonomous. Actually, it seems the opposite of the independence ideal, for they have less freedom as to when to marry.

Furthermore, long and short courtships are *both* associated with late marriage, thus forming an U-shaped curve with respect to length of courtship (x-axis) and marriage age (y-axis). Long court-ships are often expected for late marriers, who might spend years waiting for material circumstances to fall into place. On the other hand, the reasons for a short courtship and late marriage are not immediately apparent. Such relatively brief courtships might be understandable for those who marry early, as they might not have much of a chance at courtship if the socially accepted age of dating is fairly high. Yet, short courtship can also be understandable in the lives of people who have already spent a number of years saving money *before* courtship; dating, engagement, and marriage can all be temporally close together in these cases. In addition, because of their older age, they might wish to hasten the process before the 'door is closed'.

Of course, economic factors are not entirely responsible for deci-sions related to marriage. *Within the family household, there are strong influences that affect perceptions.* For example, siblings tend to affect one another in the area of marriage age, where if one marries late, they will all tend to do so. Such cross-influences oper-ate within a neighbourhood community as well. Other factors that affect marriage age in other nations, such as education and income of parents and of the couple, have little influence in Madrid.

Perhaps such absence of effect is due to the possibility that em-phases on education and income are more a function of a modern lifestyle, and consequently they have little bearing in a culture based on traditional values, even though these factors are in the process of becoming important social components.

Here we see in operation a number of traditional, probably cen-turies old, dynamics: The care in selecting a mate, the desire for an independent residence, the steadfast amassing of resources, the putting aside of marriage considerations in order to support the family, and perhaps a group dynamic effect on the propensity to marry. There are some new considerations, however: The longer wait to have a 'modern' standard of living, the lower involvement of family members in the couple's relationship, and the lesser importance attached to the economic necessity of children. A *compromise* is reached, wherein people experience independence and conviviality during youth, but plan on having a comfortable, stable home after marriage; these pursuits, however, are put aside or modified when other more substantial issues arise. They are willing to make sacrifices, balancing their own needs with the needs of others, whether they are family or friends. Thus, individuals ostensibly are committed, for the good of themselves and the community, to making the right decisions about choice of spouse, choice of residence, finances, and material standards. This dynamic occurs without much objection, and individuals, despite breathing in the modern atmosphere of independence, are prepared sometimes to go through long courtships (even if they do not call it that). In this way, they hope to achieve the goals of minimising friction within the family by discharging their filial obligations, and at the same time, living with a spouse whom they truly respect.

Madrid is an example of a modern society being able to *integrate* traditional and modernistic demands. The discipline does exist in a general population to rationally balance individual and group needs. Of course, this particular mix of ideas is more common in regions still accepting long-standing customs and Christian beliefs, and cannot be assumed to exist in the areas of Europe where there is only a tenuous attachment to the cautious, introverted temperament of forbears. Moreover, these changes seem to affect women more than men. The role of outside work in a woman's life is related, to a certain extent, to the support of her family of origin, and also to saving for marriage. It is assumed that women will not have to work after children are born, but this depends on the material needs and expectations of the household.

The truth is that the ideal of companionship is not difficult to reach, if practical, logical methods are used, and *material as well as psychological factors are taken into account.* Sporer (2010A) examined the historical process of building relationships from a traditional standpoint, and concluded that it was not an unusual occurrence for people to have very happy, contented marriages in the past. But how does a person build his or her attitudes to marriage, within the forum of powerful modern forces and processes?

As far as drawing from the well of traditional thinking, we can say that modern processes do not consciously utilise pre-modern concepts. During the 20th century, attachment to traditional values, religious belief and spiritually related activity declined significantly, and now the connection is longer relevant to many people. The path carefully laid out by European Christian teaching, where different social roles could be carefully accommodated and integrated, has given way, in post-traditional times, to a confusing array of choices based in convenience, not function. Simply put, there is presently *more fragmentation in thinking about social roles*. This is especially true for women. For example, women with little or no religious belief are *more* likely to be in the labour force, and they are more likely to never marry.[7] However, men behave opposite to that of women: The lower the level of belief amongst men, the *less* their participation in the work force.[8] In addition, the nonreligious were more likely to engage in uncommitted, sexually open relationships, than the religious.[9] Consequently, the rejection of traditional values by women, such as refusing to become a member of a church, or refusing to believe in God, leads to a resistance to other conventional concepts, such as the importance of family and supposed dependence on a man; this in turn spurs a desire for independence, and so, necessitates participation in the work force. Further, as family life, and the instruction of children, often demand submitting oneself to a moral regimen derived from Christianity, there is even less desire for women uninterested in religious matters to marry.

Despite the rhetoric from certain groups about 'having it all', the evidence shows that many women feel they have two *separate* courses laid out before them: Married life or career. They feel they must fully and intensively pursue one or the other, but not together, or even in sequence. In addition, blurring the boundaries of these roles appears to be acceptable. One could see this as a wholesale *rejection* of conventions about men's and women's roles, a choice to live without marriage, children or other commitments, in a free and easy 'Bohemian life', outside the social mainstream. But it is more likely, that this is an attempt to *sever* the conventional links between home, business, moral values, spiritual belief and success in larger society. Each area, it is now believed, can now be experienced independently, and in whatever combination or order one chooses. For example, a woman might have children out of wedlock, then pursue a career for several years during which time she lives with a man, then she starts college, at which time she lives alone again. There is in this pattern no desire to leave society or to be marginalised, yet there is the desire to fulfill different roles at different times, thus leading to cohabitation and illegitimacy. Instead of finding fulfilment in these varied roles by experiencing them in a *particular order* (education, career, marriage, children), it is thought that one can move freely in the material, external social world, and at the same time experience the various aspects of married life. In short, a major redefinition of roles has occurred.

The modern 'mentality' is not in accordance with the strategy followed by European women for centuries, and therefore, it elicits justifiable anxiety. Current thinking encourages an *abandonment* of the ideals concerning home, marriage and the economic bases for the household. In the past, the expected life timeline had *benefits* that were manifestly obvious; it was not mere custom that held people to a particular course. The heart of the confusion in modern times might very well be in calculating the *overall value* (the net worth after subtracting liabilities from the assets) of working outside the home.

Traditional women and non-traditional women both see the

necessity of being in the labour force, but clearly for different reasons. Whereas the nullifidian works as a way of achieving a highly personal, unique combination of standards, the religious person works because she wishes to attain *both* a traditional and modern set of values. Both types of women use a career to establish themselves materially, but each type also has another reason for doing so: One does so in order to attain a *juxtaposition* of 'custom-made' roles, whereas the other does so to avoid a *clash* between two traditionally defined roles.

Very often, the non-traditional want to create a life that is entirely suited to their desires, by minimising restrictions and sacrifices; their motto might be 'I will do what I wish, when I wish, in whatever way I wish, and no one can tell me otherwise'. On the other hand, those who welcome secular and religious European traditions for the invaluable assistance and edification they offer in finding contentment, will be careful to respect roles that come from these traditions. Religious, traditionally-minded women are bound to do better in life than the nullifidians, as they accept the *discipline* that comes from traditional wisdom.

However, waiting for each role to occur in succession does produce certain problems. Women might have to wait years to marry before they are settled in a career, and have adequate financial resources. Marriage within their own socioeconomic class might not be possible for these women, as the choice of partner is relatively limited for those who wait until their thirties to find a husband, a situation which necessitates going outside of a familiar social environment. Such a marriage might not be ideal in terms of personality, but if the other aspects of this lifestyle are well-planned, then there are, at least, fewer grounds for spousal disputes.

Men might be also affected by these cultural and structural factors, but they are probably less conscious about segmentation and delineation, such as the one between 'modern' and 'traditional'.

However, men are more like women in matters that pertain to standard of living, such as finances and housing, with the result that both sexes might be reluctant to marry earlier in life when they do not have a stable career or good earnings. But why might individuals refrain from marriage when they are proceeding skilfully in well-paid careers? One might say: If you have the money, and a favourably disposed companion, why not go ahead and marry?

The answer to this question lies more in the domain of psychology than culture. People who do well in their careers might find that the exacting standards that they require for work do not translate well to home life. Although rigorous and demanding demeanour is an asset for success in work, it becomes a disaster when dealing with friendships. As men and women become closer, the demands that one person makes on the other might become too onerous. It is not surprising to learn that individuals who have been unsuccessful in finding a marriage partner usually fail to form meaningful relationships because of great rigidity and low sociability.[10] Since women, in particular, feel they must compete and are often afraid of losing their position or power, they might *overcompensate* by being rigid in instructions to co-workers, never satisfied with their work, or unrealistic in setting schedules. It is likely that this carries over into private life where living with someone else can become intolerable.

Hence, single people in high stress occupations are not unaware of the potential for 'contaminating' the home environment with the problems that arise at work. Dealing with difficult people in difficult situations all day induces a certain distaste for human relations in general. Unless one has a strong belief that one will have an especially sympathetic spouse and children, one is tempted to continue living alone. Stress contagion is not an uncommon occurrence that many couples experience, where the conflicts and overload of work influences the occurrence of conflict in the home. Overemphasis on schedules, unrealistic demands, could precipitate quarrel-ling, with the tendency to converge attention on a small number of areas. In reviewing a study of home life, it is found that males, somewhat more than females, transfer arguments from work to home, and the former much more than the latter shift conflict from home to work. Furthermore, major issues of contention arise in the married household fairly frequently. Men claimed they had argu-ments with their wife or their child about once every three weeks, whereas women (perhaps more accurately) reported conflict about once every two weeks.[11]

Thus, the expansion of occupational responsibilities, and the complexification of work patterns in the latter half of the 20th century—which present challenges so different from the demands of traditional labour—have no doubt contributed to the present difficult climate at home. Not only does overwork, in general, tend to bring familial disruption, but certain occupational duties might exacerbate the tensions. This is more of an issue for women, it would appear, whose roles have an effect on how much stress they experience. For example, although female clergy experience less stress than the general population, they are more likely to experi-ence role overload than male clergy. The former perceive more stress, and believe they have fewer personal resources than males.[12]

In such circumstances, it becomes understandable why certain individuals might not wish to marry, when the unpleasant likeli-hood arises that struggles that originate in the office will continue at home, and that unresolved differences at home will exacerbate tensions at work. For the harried full-time worker, an empty home might become an oasis of peace, indeed, perhaps the only one.

These modern aspects—doubts about whether one can devote enough time to both married life and career, uncertainty about the value of work, the consequences of stress in the workplace on relationships—present many difficulties in constructing a viable developmental course for a permanent intimate relationship, a type which people desire after becoming disenchanted with the modern 'substitutes' of easy, and numerous but shallow friendships. The individual, in his quest for a positive, constructive, and rewarding companionate relationships, must discover the ways in which the material and practical aspects of life affect, and interact with, the *emotional and psychological*. In this way, he can proceed more effectively in the quest to reach his ideal, since he has attained a functional balance between the two areas.

We might express these concepts more visually, by saying that the material aspects create the 'dimensions' to a relationship, within which the psychological and emotional aspects can develop, much as a flower must exist in the correct soil placed in the proper container, otherwise it will not reach its full potential.

Although there are many ways to consider social relations, we believe that this discussion would be best served if we focus on the concept of *proximity*. As every tie has two points, there must be *distance* between these points. Distance, in the social sense, means the *level* of closeness, closeness or imminence—physical and emotional—that a person feels towards someone else, and how this positively or negatively affects his outlook on relationships in general, and on marriage in particular. Within the family of a husband, wife and children are numerous lines of connection, that vary and change in different situations, and that, no doubt, have enduring and substantial effects on all concerned. Thus, in seeking to understand the links that exist between individuals, we will pay special attention to the structure of the household of origin, as a way to understand the material and psychological considerations given to marriage. The most critical attainment in the household of childhood, within the confines or boundaries of a residence, is the *knowledge* about the ties that can bind two people together.

Expressing the idea of connectivity by social distance is well-known in sociology, yet this factor is rarely studied in relation to the development of individuality, concomitant with the pursuit of intimate relationships. Nonetheless, as evidence mounts that many, if not most, intimate relationships are deteriorating, there has never been a better opportunity to uncover and understand those dimly-perceived family dynamics, experienced early in life, which affect the individual's thinking in relation to dating, intimacy and marriage.

Consequently, in this book, we will examine the concepts, patterns, and dynamics of *contemporary material aspects of life* that can possibly help or hinder the individual in his desire to reach his ideal of companionship, by focussing on how the material and pragmatic affect the psychological and emotional. So far, we have discovered that these challenges were known to our European ancestors; certain areas of the concept of companionship have changed. This is easily seen in the selfish development of the 'pragmatic' side of relationships, where one seeks out a person of the opposite sex for personal enhancement, but is not necessarily prepared to give consideration and sacrifice. However, other areas have remained as they have been, continuing to hold traditional ideas, as where general concepts about integrating personality and material concerns have remained unscathed by the sharp sword of modernism. We will continue to pay attention to this phenomenon of traditional concepts remaining relevant, even to the present day, as well as to further develop the other issues discussed above, and to trace out their consequences.

Chapter 2

Considerations
of Marriage

*F*rom the evidence we have presented so far, one can see that the demands of education and career have largely dissolved the long-standing traditional organic associations between marriage, finances, career, and intimacy. Nevertheless, there is still a link between two areas that many people believe *should be maintained*, namely that of marriage and children. In the Western world, it is widely thought that the decision to have children should be made by a man and woman who are married; however, this is taken further, in that many believe the decision to marry should at least partly be based on the desire to have children.

Indeed, there are pragmatic reasons, which relate to emotional concerns, as to why people would want children, as children provide easy social contact. Children provide special social and emotional benefits that cannot be fulfilled by others, apart perhaps from a spouse. The loss of essential links with the world is far more likely for people who do not have children than for people with children. Only about one in ten of people with children has not had any social contact in the last day or two, but far more people without children, about one in four, have difficulty in establishing meetings and communications with others. Although childless individuals might fraternise with others as compensation, they do *not* see family, friends or neighbours more often. Such isolation is particularly strong for those in poor health, and from manual labour/working class backgrounds.[13] No matter how independent one might be at earlier ages, one cannot easily countenance such 'autonomy' in old age, when sympathetic support from others is imperative. Older men and woman without children and living alone are more likely to be socially isolated, i.e. without any face-to-face contact with others. Those in poor health and others with special needs are particularly dependent on close relatives, who, more than others, feel obligated to tolerate the emotional and physical strains. Being a member of a social class that is outside the mainstream economically and educationally makes it even more difficult to reach out; fear of ridicule and criticism often makes for an insular mentality that limits social interaction to a small network of dependable kin. It is clear that, whether or not one likes to entertain the idea, isolation in old age is significantly more likely if one has no children. That isolation can even be nightmarish if one is childless *and* unmarried.

Companionship, however, is not the only reason that one has children, as many can expect a spouse to serve in this capacity well into old age. Children bring many rewards to couples, who fulfill their destiny as nurturers and contributors to mankind. Son and daughters have always satisfied deep emotional desires, by bringing a sense of purpose to life, by giving one the opportunity to impart guidance and knowledge, and by perpetuating the family name. In addition, they could serve to aid in occupational and household chores. Thus, children bring emotional and material components to family life. They help to lay out tangible 'dimensions' to a household, which in turn furnish enduring solidity to married life.

But many nowadays seem to purposely ignore these facts, and their potential needs in later life; children form an unnecessary adjunct in a society obsessed with superficial pursuits, autonomy and youth. Those couples without children, far from seeing children as a path to consummation of their roles, see them as *impediments* to self-actualisation; they instead look for fulfilment through education and career. In fact, such couples see children as creating nothing less than a threat to marital harmony.[14]

No longer do children bring the kinds of rewards they did in the past, and for those who desire to be childless, marital life has been transformed. Many couples see marriage only as a public certification of their relationship and little else. The 'growth of the self' within marriage is often facilitated through external factors, not necessarily through the activities within the household.

Actually, the pressure to have children, just as the pressure to marry, whether acknowledged or not, might now be *more* extensive than in the past. Because of the demands of the industrial economy, many feel an obligation to contribute to society by providing new members. The insistence by the present culture on families and individuals to achieve the age's promise is great. Their son or daughter might be the researcher who discovers a cure for a devastating disease, the astronaut who lands on Mars, the President that finally eliminates the nuclear threat in the world, or the scientist who develops a cheap form of fuel. Married couples have assimilated a concept that they must provide the human resources that will maintain and complete the arduous struggle for material 'perfection'—a concept that is the product of the curious, spiritless view of the world that began in the 18th century. However, this duty to continue the improvement of the physical well-being of society does not exempt spouses from 'self-actualising', and they can only feel exasperated by costly and incongruous social requirements, without being able to identify clearly the source of those demands.

Looked at from a larger perspective, the modern person is still burdened by various constraints or requirements. Yet the average individual has more freedom in the personal domain than in the past. Some demands, as in the case of having children, are relatively untouched by time, but other demands no longer exist, yet have been replaced by others. The key factors, which encouraged or discouraged matrimony for our ancestors, are no longer pertinent. Clearly, inheritance is no longer a major factor in acquiring the financial basis for a household or setting up a business. Few people are constrained by the terms of their employment, such as was the case with those in domestic service, apprenticeships or farm labour. Marriage markets are generally balanced, and few regions experience major in-migration or out-migration. In this improved social situation, ideals about companionship, married life and male-female intimacy are allowed to flourish and are thought much more attainable. The focus can now be more on personality factors in the search for a relationship, and a longer term view of the successful establishment of a household. There are more personal, and less pragmatic, factors being taken into account. Nonetheless, freedom from stringent material criteria does not mean that pragmatic factors are unimportant; it is still plausible that economic conditions substantially affect the desirability of marriage from the individual's viewpoint.

Is this lesser dependence on material factors realistic? At the beginning of the chapter, it was stated that changes in Western society have de-linked associations between certain life areas. However, we have shown here that the association between children and marriage still remains strong: The pressure to attain one domain brings pressure to attain the other. We can therefore see that, as children are often part of a larger economic 'enterprise', and since the husband and wife are chiefly responsible in setting up a household, with relatives not usually having critical roles, it would stand to reason that the couple would take the greatest care in assuring the *continuing material viability of a family unit containing themselves and their children*. Through long experience, mankind has come to understand that when financial troubles cloud the horizon, it is very difficult to maintain a happy household, and such pecuniary difficulties are, not surprisingly, one of the top reasons given for divorce.[15] Thus, material factors still exert great influence, due to the social expectation that the couple will have children.

There is no doubt marriage can act as a way of improving one's financial situation, by reducing expenses, reducing taxes, and pooling income. In the past, this desire for efficiency translated to a general inclination against division of wealth, households and property. Traditional wisdom affirmed that, unless some overweening economic factor compensated for the inefficiency, the splitting of a household was an unquestionably imprudent action for people of limited means:

. . . since it would be necessary to place two cloths on two tables, to burn two logs in two hearths, to hire two servants for two households, where only one is needed.[16]

The 15th century writer who wrote these words was referring not only to a married household, but any household where people share accommodations, such as brothers and sisters living together. In contrast to the modern centrifugal forces, traditional society felt *centripetal* movement, towards collectivity, towards the centre, and towards cooperation. Hence, marriage was not the only manner in which the traditional ideal of economic efficiency could be accomplished, but through any one of a myriad of other forms of living arrangements that brought or kept people together. In this scenario, marriage was seen as a positive development in the economic sense. But the trend in Western culture has been towards forging a *self-made course*, where privacy and self-dominion prevails. What seemed reasonable in the slowly unfolding societies of the Middle Ages and Renaissance, did not seem acceptable in a strongly growing economy, where the production of cloth, food, furniture, and other necessary items for new households was becoming more efficient.

Flexibility and opportunity in modern society have eradicated certain old problems, but have produced new stresses, such as the common belief that one must continually attempt to reach a higher 'quality of life'. Because of this 'consumerist' culture, one that demands constant upgrading, people of the modern era still look to optimise their financial situation, but unlike the past, where relatives could live with one another in order to reduce expenses, in the present time, household fusion is common only through marriage. Thus, any consideration of long-term money management must take into account marriage plans, and any decisions about marriage should take into account the effects of those decisions on personal expenses; the areas of finance and married life have become tightly bound up with each other.

Independence from economic burdens is more critical than independence from people, for a relationship can be more easily modified than material matters. Money quite simply brings independence in any society, at any time, and food, housing, clothing, and other items are consequential. Accordingly, a fuller appreciation of household financial management must consider, as in any enterprise, all sources of revenues, or inflow of funds, as well as possible costs, or outflow of funds.

Therefore, we ask: How do expenses figure in the decision to marry? It is evident people will want to forestall marriage if they feel that their revenues (from work, inheritance, savings, and so on) will not be adequate for the life they have envisioned. But what about changing the age of marriage because *expenses* are simply too high? Clearly in this instance, we are talking about factors largely outside the control of the individual. The specific monetary factors of conjugal life have been little researched and are thus difficult to follow. What we wish to know here is whether an analysis of international data can validate the idea, that the *ability* to obtain important items, such as a house, car, furniture, or appliances, also affects the age of marriage. Data for such items is sparse, and we have only general categories to follow, i.e. food, durable goods, entertainment, personal items. However, our analysis reveals that the *higher* the cost of domestic variables such as food, clothing, household durables, and the *lower* the cost of housing and recreation, the likelier that a woman, at least, will marry *early*.[17] Let us investigate these issues further.

As a general principle, the establishment of a modern economy invariably involves the loss of time for household tasks, and so one of the first priorities of such an economy is to make available cheap goods and services. Food, clothing, domestic articles and durables are the basic items of any household and a higher cost for these items would entail marrying early as a way of reducing the costs of these items through various means. A man and woman might have a greater tendency to move directly to a marital abode from the parental home, if living alone was simply too expensive. If people find that they are better off marrying early in order to reduce expenses, then they are more tied to a particular place and have less time to give for a career. One way to reduce costs is through consolidation of expenses; understandably, sharing the same furnishings would be less expensive than having the same kinds of items in two different households. Another way would be to take advantage of a woman's domestic skills and capabilities. Previous generations knew that women were invaluable in the household, as expressed in the rather unrefined English saying, 'the wife that expects to have a good name, is always at home, as if she were lame'. She could knit or sew, reducing or eliminating the expense of buying clothes. A wife could also cook both for herself and her husband, freeing the latter from the bachelor's burden of having to cook for himself, or from taking the expensive route of dining out. Even though the orientation to perform domestic duties is cultural, the high value of a wife who can perform these functions is universal. Such a woman would be quickly 'snapped up' by men who are concerned about living expenses.

As there is evidently a wider variation in food costs than in the past, the cost of such items is a determining factor in the decision to marry. Where food is relatively expensive, fewer resources are available for other activities, and the amount a household spends on food is positively related to the probability a woman will marry early. In the earlier history of domestic life, edibles were almost always prepared at home using basic ingredients, whereas in our day, food can be prepared easily in a restaurant, fast-food shop, or factory. It is expedient to have at least one family member manage provisions and cook in the household, in nations where food is relatively expensive, in order to preserve funds. Where food is efficiently grown and processed by companies, the extra amount added, due to labour, does not make the total cost exorbitant. Accordingly, the home budget, in nations with relatively cheap food, permits more dining out, as well as the buying of mass-produced items which require only simple processing.

Other costs can act to facilitate or non-facilitate marriage. In relation to the pre-Industrial era, when more money is available for entertainment expenses, young men and women will have numerous divertissements and amusements that act as suitable alternatives to married life, which in turn lowers the marriage age. One reason this money might become more available is on account of lower food expenses. Entertainment acts as an alternative to the gratification of married life, but only an approximate one since there can be no direct substitution of the essence of conjugal existence. Yet, if entertainment is cheaper, age of marriage is not increased but *lowered*. Although young single people in many cities still enjoy entertainment as an alternative to marriage,[18] and have satisfactory emotional outlets in this manner, it would appear that this activity is often used in service of a higher purpose: To date and to court. Thus, recreation does not really act as a *substitute* for married life in our day, but as a means to getting married. Leisure activities are important components of a young person's budget, as often meeting friends and dating are tied together and indeed revolve around expensive diversions. If recreation is expensive, then the dating experience becomes more difficult, and this in turn makes it less likely that a person will marry early. This is perhaps in contrast with earlier periods, where the enjoyment of cheap entertainment would *forestall* marriage (i.e. a positive correlation between early marriage and recreation expenses).

Housing in particular has an important role to play in marital dynamics; it has a positive correlation with marriage age, indicating that a lower cost of housing entails an earlier marriage, and a higher cost delays marriage. Lower residential expenses therefore facilitate the formation of a conjugal household. However, people can adjust to circumstances if the need for marriage is high and costs remain intractable. A couple might marry and then live with one spouse's parents because buying or renting a residence is simply too expensive, even if both husband and wife work full-time. If the costs are far too high, or availability is extremely limited, then they might actually forego the idea of creating their own separate household, and simply take over the running of the household when one or both parents die. We shall cover housing and various related issues in more detail later on.

Although the negative correlation between housing cost and marriage age is still traditional, the other relationships are not. A higher cost of food would ordinarily have meant a decrease in real income, followed by a *decline* in nuptiality.[19] Perhaps the modern household is able to save more money if the occupants are married, but this thwarts social independence as people decide to pursue love instead. Out of the three choices of living arrangements that people had in the past—live with family, live alone, live with spouse—the cost of living with a spouse (and probably children) was highest, followed by living alone, and the cheapest was living with one's family. There was often no choice in the matter of food, clothing, and furniture; most of it was made at home, borrowed or handed down. In whichever of the three living situations, it was a case of 'do it yourself' in order to survive. Thus, the question then became whether marriage was reasonable, as the three, four, or more children that would be added to a couple's own household might be more than they could handle. In the present day, where people can make things at home or buy them ready made, clearly it is cheaper to share. Since the size of a married household does not have to grow by very much, if at all, (since fertility being much lower than in the past), then one would prefer to marry instead of staying at home, thereby fulfilling the ideal of love, as well as effecting a sound financial design.

Taken together, we see how various essential items in the household budget could have a major effect on the decision to marry. Nonetheless, we might envision a situation reverse to that portrayed above: Instead of expenses affecting marriage age, marriage age affects the economy, and that in turn affects the household expenses. When it becomes a general practise within a society to marry early, young adults will have their liberty limited, and the economy then becomes less flexible and less viable. Further, as more women marry young, their contribution to the work force declines, which in turn hinders the development of technology, and increases the cost of basic items, such as food. How might this happen? Such women might relinquish the idea of higher education and take jobs requiring lesser mental ability but greater physical effort. Companies will have this segment of the work force available for cheaper labour and eschew more advanced technology. Thus, the economy is forced to continue using expensive methods to produce food and other products instead of advancing in that field. To reach this conclusion, however, seems premature, as the connections between women's age at marriage, work, and production are not well-defined.

At this point, the evidence we have collected shows that the design of living arrangements is substantively affected by material considerations. This consideration is not often openly discussed, as it would clash with both the commitment to 'personal freedom', and the avowal that 'we can live on love alone'. *Economics still maintains a critical influence on the decisions one makes in relation to companionship, and the individual's perceived level of freedom is probably not accurate.* However, this lessening of independence has been allowed to occur by the individual himself, and has not been forced upon him.

Besides expenses, one must look at the other side of the ledger, that of *income.* External variables continue to affect the decision to marry, especially a woman's assessment of the potential future earnings of her husband and the economic stability of a married household. Based upon an analysis of Western nations, multicorrelation reveals that the most important variables in association with late life celibacy (never marrying) are income per capita, concentration of wealth, and proportion of the male population in the workforce.[20] These factors bear closer examination.

Even though people might *claim* that, for them personally, there is no strong connection between material factors and the decision to marry, evidence shows that income considerations continue to have a prominent role, in a way consistent with the factors that have played a major role in the past. Further research points to specific economic aspects which can play a *very* important role. Whether a husband is firmly employed (whether he is a dedicated member of the labour force) is highly salient; his employment is undoubtedly critical in a functioning household, and so in a happy marriage. Lack of employment and difficulty holding a job might be attributed to a variety of male figures a woman knows: Father, brother, uncle, or some other relative. Recognising among her family members a limited career potential, few employment opportunities and/or a general indolence towards work might make a woman hold an unfavourable view of marriage.

Although a single woman might make a good living by working within the 'female' areas of the labour force, the more complex enterprise of marriage, which involves higher material demands and children, must be supported for the most part by the earnings of the husband. Any interruptions in this most essential and irreplaceable cash flow might spell disaster; women would wisely want to assure the dependability of this resource, before embarking on an enterprise that operates so close to the 'break-even point'.

For similar reasons, a lower income also prompts putting off marriage, as some women, found all across the socioeconomic scale, would then believe it would be difficult to achieve the specific material level that they have clearly visualised. This level, interestingly, although ostensibly personal, might be derived from an international standard; years of societal cross-influencing has created what could be called the 'prototypical household,' containing particular types of television, telephone, washing machine, dishwasher, car, etc. Thus, a similar 'visualisation' would be applicable in poorer countries such as Portugal, as well as in wealthier ones such as Germany. However, more research is necessary before the dynamics involved can be properly elucidated.

A greater concentration of wealth, where income is in the hands of a few people in the upper echelons of society, also induces an avoidance of marriage and encourages permanent celibacy (see Sporer 1999). Women might see a clear disparity in earnings in the local environment, such as a divergence between upper management and everyone else in her department or company. One could achieve middle managerial status and still not achieve a significantly better income; earning power of a high calibre rests in the hands of the special class of executives and professionals. Such an observation might force the conclusion that the nation's businesses *do not reward merit or hard work*, but simply pull people up through the ranks using an 'old boy network'. The expectation in the modern world is that advancement in position is met by a commensurate advancement in income, and if this is not the case, then, in the minds of some women, a future married household could not achieve the standard of living that was envisioned, no matter how hard-working they are. If the expectation is for a husband and wife to have children, as there normally is, then they must assume that increased work will cause an expansion in income, covering the expenses incurred by all members of the family. If this expansion in income cannot occur because of a failure to reward merit, then marriage itself is considered to be not worthwhile, as the family would undergo a *reduction* in living standard after children are born; the parents have reached a ceiling in income, and every child that is added to the household can only bring down the standard of living per person. This would probably be more of a factor for women who are sensitive to issues of fairness, who have faith in the merit-reward system, who are ambitious and work hard, who believe that living standards should only increase, and who believe that married life inevitably entails having children.

In the United States, the growing income *inequality* between households in recent years is attributed to a number of factors: Declining unionisation; paying premiums for skilled labour; a shift from goods-producing to service-producing industries (wherein a *greater* disparity in incomes exists); and a change in living arrangements, away from married couple households, to single parent and other types of household.[21] This last aspect is especially relevant to our investigation, although the *direction* of causality is opposite to what we expect. There is no doubt that more people living alone or single causes greater inequality, since the earning power of a smaller household will usually be smaller than that of a larger household. However, we also have no doubt that the distribution of income influences the decision to marry. We can conclude that this variable is probably *bidirectional*, in that it is related to permanent celibacy as both a cause and an effect. It validates the belief that a woman living on her own would probably earn less income than if living in a two-person household. We would in this case be saying that the relationship is obverse to the one cited above, that non-marriage leads to *more* inequality rather than the other way around.[22]

We have seen that economic and material considerations, components that make up the 'dimensions' of a relationship, continue to be, as in the past, vitally important in marital assessment and planning. In traditional times, the successful attainment of the material aspects of individual and family life, of balancing expenses and income, was dependent on obtaining domestic skills, a certain amount of good fortune, and sincere cooperation between people. There is little doubt that a man or woman living in the modern industrial society has his or her marital prospects resting precariously on achieving a variety of 'successes' in life, such as obtaining a college diploma, moving into a higher level occupation, attaining promotions, networking with capable and experienced people, even overcoming various social inequities. The complex interaction of these forces, compared to a century ago, might have a disproportionate share of impact on a couple's relationship. Thus, a man's, or woman's manner of dealing with people, money, career and so on are added to the list of important traits that need to be evaluated. A failure in any one regard could be the kiss of death for the relationship; accomplishment in the outside world is confused and alloyed with proficiency in the inner world of domestic life.

What is even more disturbing is that these materialistic evaluations could be wrong. It is true that those who have a high education probably will have developed persistence and discipline, as completion of a college degree requires success at every stage in the process. But studies show that early academic success does *not* assure later success, although early academic failure strongly predicts later failure. Still, even after experiencing early failures, some people can attain a high level of education.[23] Further, high school students' hoped for or expected future earnings are very weakly correlated with actual earnings.[24]

Consequently, *if the individual is using success in education as a predictor of success in career,* the chance of error is substantial. The use of education as an indicator of marriage partner suitability is astute, but only when such a method is allied with knowledge of its limitations.

We should note that the issues we have raised here rarely appear in public discourse. In a curious twist, when addressing marriage experts and authorities often completely fail to mention the material issues relating to that institution, instead focussing on the emotional dynamics that move the relationship towards union. The current rhetoric about marriage being fundamentally a product of 'romantic' motivations does not take into account the fact that for there to be love and affection, there must also be security, stability, and predictability; only the proper, intelligent handling of financial opportunities can assure the material grounding of emotional fulfilment. Therefore, in public discourse, commentators cannot broach the subject of the economic aspects that contribute to marriage, without having to face, at some point, the emotionless and self-centred ambition that often is required in obtaining material 'success'. For a modernist, it is better to say nothing at all on the subject, than to be dragged into acknowledging society's many faults.

We should consider whether, when evaluating a person's character, it is fair or appropriate to put such great weight on the attributes of a person's career or education. Where complex economic factors merge with complex personal motivations in the modern world, there is no easy association between achievement in one area, with achievement in another. Is there any reason to presume that a well-educated man in an executive position would be a better husband any more than a man well down the ladder in the same company? Assembling the various components requires deftness and skill; on that basis, *social competence* appears to 'set up' the pragmatic material aspects. Since we have determined that the level of dexterity with which a person handles his environment has a substantial effect on his relationships, let us now examine them more closely, and untwine the complex factors that constitute social competence.

Chapter 3

Social Competence and Aptitude

*C*onsiderations about the future necessarily entail evaluating a person's marriageability, and we are essentially focussing on *proficiency* in making friends, dealing with challenges, gaining academic credentials, attaining career prestige, and earning a satisfactory income. It is widely thought that a socially capable individual will do well in a career through his ability to make profitable personal contacts, and a scholastically-inclined person will also do well in a career by virtue of his academic credentials. Knowing the interaction between these factors would be of great help, yet the *magnitude* and *sequence of causality* of these factors are often difficult to determine. For example, does education determine marriage age or the other way around? Does education have a critical role to play in career, prestige or income? The multifarious interactions of these factors demand careful examination, and the best understanding is reached when individuals are followed over a period of time, preferably from teenage years to mid-life.

We are fortunate in having such a longitudinal study, as described by Willits (1988). It is unusual for its size and span of time, giving us considerable insight into the personality, group, material and educational influences that go into decisions about marriage in the 20th century. More than 2800 sophomores, at 74 rural high schools, were given a questionnaire in 1947, followed by another questionnaire in 1984 (at around age 55), the latter being given to all former students who could be found. The number of people finally assessed was 1,650, thus providing scholars with an unprecedented opportunity to study the development of life paths.

We can see that a number of points are evident from this study. Firstly, there is a fairly strong positive correlation between peer relations and family relations. Evidently, the family prepares the individual for larger society. In those households where children learn how to deal with others cordially, intelligently and dependably at an early age, they are capable of using these skills with non-family members later on. Not surprisingly, there is also an explicit positive correlation between peer relations and opposite sex relations. This would indicate that, when one is able to deal with friends on a non-romantic basis, one is also able to enjoy good relations with a boyfriend or girlfriend; it appears that learning to get along with people, in general, secures certain abilities that produce satisfying dating and courtship experiences.

However, aptitude with peers does not appear to link with an aptitude for education. Whereas good grades and participation in formal organisations tend to lead to higher educational attainment, good relations with peers had *no* significant correlation with attainment. Doing well with friends does little in the process of gaining an education, but extracurricular activities and certainly high grades have a definite influence on the way people progress through the layers of pedagogical experience. It is well known that school administrators and college admission boards often assess an individual by both grades and social activities, so it is not surprising that such a relationship exists. Further, success with peers has a positive effect on later family income and well-being, and popularity with members of the opposite sex generally has a *negative* correlation with education, though not with occupational prestige. The popular young man or woman who does well in dating will likely have many good prospects for marriage, leading to earlier matrimony, with its associated adult responsibilities suspending or delaying higher college attendance. Hence, this situation does not bode well for one's educational course as plans might have to be put off or forgone if being married is of higher priority.

Thus, concerns about companionship often come *before* marked interest in education and income; some might find the fulfilment of spouse and family more important than external social considerations. There are those who seek a more secure and warm protector than current trends, which are subject to constant revision and debate. Indeed, in the traditional conception of things, one puts one's faith in what one can see and touch. As Chaucer acknowledged, a wife is more important than wisdom, and a *good* wife is the greatest accomplishment a man can have. In this, he echoes Proverbs 31:10 (NRSV), which states: 'A capable wife who can find? She is far more precious than jewels'. The results of the Willits study suggest that such a philosophy is not only sentimental, but pragmatic as well, for popularity with the opposite sex (in addition to good relations with peers and academic performance) leads to *higher* family earnings, and *higher* subjective well-being. This is rather curious to contemporary minds, since education is believed to have an important, indeed decisive, impact on later earning capacity and standard of living. Nevertheless, as we have already discussed the fact that certain men and women have high expectations for marriage, seeing it as the most fulfilling of all relationships (page 6), it should not surprise us that many people seek great competence in a spouse. Among the factors that govern well-being, education must stand along with choice of a spouse. The reason is this: A popular young man, with high ideals, might have contacts with many girls, and so he has the advantage of a large potential marriage partner pool, from which he would obviously choose the most resourceful, intelligent, and capable woman. Clearly, such a wife might have a good earning capacity of her own, and she might find ways to save money on household expenses. In this way, the ideal of companionship can be fulfilled.

The most important, as well as the most puzzling, aspect of our analysis concerns the relationship between education, social activities and peer relations, since these three areas are so crucial to the conceptualisation of autonomy and independence. Educational achievement is positively correlated with school activities, whereas the former is not related to success with peer relations. If one is good at social activities, would one be good at peer relations? Evidently so, for school activities and peer relations *are* positively related. The individual might spend time with peers, which might increase his participation in activities, or the other way around. Whichever the case, his satisfying casual associations do not have an impact on his education, but do sometimes put him in the midst of constructive social activities of a more formal nature, which gives him the opportunity to display competence and leadership. This kind of social legitimacy does have a meaningful influence on his education and career, but not necessarily on finding a spouse.

Although these associations are quite understandable, we wonder why peer relations are not related to educational attainment. There is the possibility that each area requires different skills and techniques. And so here we come to the critical question: Can one realistically expect to attain just the right combination of education, social activity, career, and companionship? In other words, can one have true social freedom and find true love as well? By way of reference to common stereotypes, most people do not appear to believe that this is possible. It is often assumed that one must focus on the 'people' track and dispense with schooling, or focus on the 'academic' track and dispense with socialising, in order for each to fully yield its rewards. This thinking, however, is flawed, as the evidence suggests that the putative connections within either 'track' might not exist at all. Thus, there is no guarantee that by following a track one will reach one's desired goals.

In relating to the issue of autonomy, Sporer (2010A) addressed the possible reasons underlying the ease or difficulty with which one engages in social relations (extroversion or introversion), and the effect that this has on the size of one's friendship circle, and the desire to marry. Genetics might determine extroversion, and this has an effect on the way people might consequently use peer relations to build companionate friendships, which can lead to marriage, or act as a substitute for marriage. Here we confront the issue of inherited traits again, but the issue is whether the track that one is on (education or career), is the result of innate (genetically determined) temperament, or the result of conscious choice. There is a definite dichotomy in the conventional thinking of young people about social roles, in that it is believed the average individual is forced to make an unequivocal *choice:* Concentrate on forming good relations with peers, *or* concentrate on attaining a good education. To put it simply, one must be either a *bon vivant* or a *bookworm*; each obtains compensation and satisfaction in the long and short term, although each is treated differently within the peer group. Yet this kind of dichotomy does not really exist within typical youth social environments. It is possible for one to be quite good at studies and still be congenial, or one can be academically inferior and also be unattractive to schoolmates.

The general consensus in Western thinking is that the individual is influenced by a predilection, and is not a slave to an all-consuming lifestyle. In line with this, it is widely believed that in a democratic modern society one can freely *choose* either track without significant interference from the outside. In the Willits study, there is no significant correlation between *peer relations* and *education*; grades and test scores still determine the lion's share of one's capabilities. This suggests that there are indeed no *clear* social or external impediments. However, impediments do exist, but they are for the most part innate or *internal*. It is true, that many who have the potential to become a bon vivant, choose to become a bookworm, and then go on to college, and one can deduce from the facts of the above study that the very different courses of bon vivant –> lesser education, or bookworm –> higher education, are not inevitable.

Most young people wish to attain the combination of conviviality, social activity, and education that is to their liking; nonetheless, the theory that one should only, or could only, pour one's energies into either the 'social' track or the 'academic' track, is erroneous. If many people were showing an unambiguous preference for one or the other, then there would be a *negative* association between peer relations and educational attainment, but this is not what we see.

Thus, using the Willits study as a guide, it is reasonable to conclude that people possess the freedom to obtain the right mix of career, education, and social activity, if they are able to live with or overcome innate limitations. Without making overly broad generalisations, it can be said that *success or failure in one course or the other is largely secured by natural aptitude, or the lack of it, and not by explicit choice or merit.* For example, one might *wish* to converge one's attention on school learning, and in the process forego peer relations, but college education might be elusive because one does not possess the required intelligence, interest, or diligence. On the other hand, an absence of positive social qualities might make one a failure in cultivating friendships, but because of the right *inherent* of genetically determined traits, one can direct one's energies through another legitimate and laudable channel, that of intellectual refinement. Furthermore, the bookworm's college education might stand him in good stead when looking for work, but there are no assurances that his education will procure the income and prestige he wants. In any case, only a subgroup of socially dextrous individuals lacks the intellectual development to go on to college, and only a subgroup of socially limited individuals possess the acumen to go on to higher education.

Hence, individuals who conform to the stereotypes 'bookworm' or 'bon vivant', although socially obvious and the focus of attention, are not numerous enough for us to turn their life experiences into a general rule.

We also find in the study that if one has success in *school social activities*, then there is an increased chance of completing *higher education*. This must also be due to *nature* since if it were a matter of *choice* one could go directly to higher education without having to take the time and effort to become involved in extracurricular activities. Due to a fortuitous combination of looks, charm, and various ineffable qualities, one is able to deepen friendships, have a good social life, and become popular with the opposite sex. This could all take place in the life of someone dedicated to academic studies, but in reality it often leads to earlier marriage with little or no tertiary level education. For whatever innate reasons, the individual might have a good relationship with peers, teachers and others in a structured school environment, which translates to a good relationship with the opposite sex, which in turn has an effect on schooling. However, when these qualities are allied with leadership ability, then social activities can act as a powerful springboard to higher education. In this case, marriage might be put off in order to fulfill the potential for higher learning.

The often heard belief that those who marry early are socially competent but not well-educated, and those who go on to college are socially awkward but obtain good qualifications and good jobs, appears to be incorrect. In reality, the former do have a path to a good living and prestige, not through education, but through likability and congeniality; in other words, through the force of *personality*. Sometimes, and rather unpredictably, they have additional characteristics that assist them in gaining a higher educational qualification. Further, the latter might not be awkward at all; getting better education is not necessarily connected to being socially isolated. Yet, those who ignore social relations and activities are the most difficult for whom to make predictions, as they do not have as estimable a course as the socially gregarious.

It should be stressed that the correlations between the variables cited from the Willits study, though significant, were not especially forceful individually, demonstrating that other factors can certainly not be excluded. Thus, *people have more freedom than believed in the sense that academics and social living are not mutually exclusive areas*, but they also have less freedom than believed in that much is determined by natural or inherent proclivities and temperament. The amount of 'freedom' that one possesses, is determined largely by one's estimation of the difficulty attending various external and internal constraints. For the person who has no problem modifying his own tendencies for the sake of achieving a goal, great personal freedom should optimistically be envisaged using the scenario we have described here. Conventional wisdom about the modern person's total freedom and total control over his life are, in this case, not consistent with the facts and should be discarded. There is some relevance to the common assumption, but it lacks refinement to the point that the truth is obscured. This realisation could seriously damage the concept of independence upon which contemporary society has placed so many of its aims.

These models concern people maturing earlier in the 20th century, when higher education was far more exclusive, and so not part of the average individual's set of life goals. A person could marry early and relinquish further education without the fear of having compromised his reputation. Nevertheless, attitudes to early marriage are not immutable. Research has found that males who marry as adolescents tend to have fewer years of education, and earn less income and hold lower-status occupations. Considering the importance of high-status as a means of acquiring respect, these lower-status persons predictably are accorded less consideration and favour compared to other men, resulting in greater marital disruption.[25] In this case, it is the early marriage that might disrupt the possibility of education and a better career.

This finding is at variance with the results derived from the study by Willits (1988), where early marriage meant *higher* income, and so higher status. It might be explained by the fact that cultural attitudes of young people in the current generation are distinctly different to those of a generation earlier. Matrimony that occurs early in life is now 'looked down upon', and the ceremony is performed, more as an 'emergency' operation, than as the natural outcome of profitable peer interaction. A difficult home life or avoiding an even worse social disgrace, namely, the birth of an illegitimate child, might impel individuals to wed as soon as possible. In addition, disruption within the marriage might stem from the frustrations of being in a lower occupation and a lower social class, and the clash of educational and social expectations. The strong expectation is for young people to finish their education, or to establish themselves in an occupation, then get married, and then have children. In the past, this sequence could be somewhat modified, as people put human relations before that of career, but today, the succession of milestones is less amenable to change, because the economy demands that a career is made as high a priority as possible.

For females, it is education, or the lack of it, that dictates marital considerations. The improvement in women's education, which brings better career opportunities, does give them the potential for greater economic independence, but this does not necessarily mean that they will greatly or permanently postpone marriage and childbearing, nor does it mean that the manifold demands of education and career will unduly disrupt relations with a husband and children. Women might delay marriage only in the transitional phase from youth to adulthood.[26]

The modern simultaneous preoccupation with independence, standard of living, and intimacy, leads sometimes to unusual life plans. Nonetheless, it is still a reasonable expectation that goals relating to education, work, and family, can be fulfilled within a reasonable time scale. *Eschewing such a sensible pattern evidently has more to do with following personal conceptions and cultural values, than being constrained by the rigid rules of peer group, school or business.* Career or education becomes a real impediment to satisfactory married life only if the individual *allows* such a condition to occur. In regard to this, people must show flexibility, since a highly predetermined life course might not be possible.

So far, we have identified the continuing importance of the concept of marriage for most people, although it is admittedly *poorly integrated with other critical life areas*, including education, career and children. This lack of integration has resulted in difficulties in assessing and maintaining the economic basis of married life. Nonetheless, the failings of conceptualisation can be *offset*, to an extent, through greater aptitude and competence at social relations, especially when education as a preparation for career is properly considered.

Further, we have raised a number of important issues concerning the establishment and maintenance of the role of husband or wife. The success in achieving this role, it can be seen, is dependent on a number of important life decisions, which relate to social competence. Previously we mentioned (page 29) that evidence continues to show that material factors, in their pivotal relation to marriage are not discussed openly today, at the educational, political, or socio-religious levels. However, what is clear is that people have become averse to following *specific pathways*, because they feel that it interferes with their liberty and freedom. Social competence begins in early life, and it continues its development through the first independent living arrangements one makes.

Clearly social competence and aptitude must be expressed in certain tangible ways. Let us now study the process of building maturity in the Western world, and see which accomplishments are important in defining this concept. In particular, we should focus on how income might affect orientation to marriage in the living situation that a person will enter upon after leaving his childhood family. Because of its relation to social competence, the issuing of a personal 'declaration of independence' determines the dimensions of future relationships and companionship within marriage. The points in one's *development cycle* at which such 'declarations' occur is possibly a critical factor in how one earns money, saves money, assumes social roles, pursues education and builds a career. As we examine this phenomenon, we should again return to address an important question in relation to Free Will and individuality: Are the decisions behind the steps to maturity largely the result of social forces, or are they the confidant exercise of personal choice?

Chapter 4

Steps to Maturity

ifestyle issues, centring around notions of adulthood, responsibility, and material standards, are often the focus of social attention. Everyone truly wants to swim 'effortlessly' through life, without major worries. Yet, for those people who strive to be 'modern', fulfilling the long list of socially prescribed requirements, especially within the middle and upper class lifestyles, is costly and exhausting. In this scenario, the almost obsessive focus on external standards creates a habit of less flexibility that makes long-term relationships difficult. Consequently, in modern society, appearances are often more important than reality. It is apparent that the actual accomplishment of becoming independent is less important than the *appearance* of being autonomous. Similarly, how much pleasure one is actually receiving from an activity is of secondary concern compared to how much pleasure one *appears* to be having. We should therefore see what 'markers' society has constructed that 'indicate' one has become independent, and at least ready for marriage.

Although numerous forces in society have coalesced to form a nearly universally accepted 'independence ethos', the contribution of individuals to this preconceived plan has been relatively weak. What is this modern 'independence ethos'? The definition is based on the concept that adeptness in handling problems in life is correlated to social status. Thus, the belief is that challenges should be accepted freely; obstacles should be negotiated using one's courage, ingenuity, and talents; and predetermined goals must be attained decisively. In other words, one must 'win the game' without enjoying major support from others. To conquer the challenge requires drawing on personal resources and skills. To fail means that, either the skills were not developed, or the individual did not draw upon them. By being in an accelerated academic course, attending an exclusive school, purchasing an expensive item, or having a difficult mission-critical job, the individual calls attention to himself; his successful handling of the situation, where others might or might not have had the same opportunity, raises his status, and earns him admiration.

One of the first steps the individual takes on the road to bringing the ethos to life, is to reside in a 'place of own's own', that is, to take on the challenge of leaving the family abode. Such a separation is difficult for both parents and their children, yet is usually inevitable. There are only two questions that need to be resolved: At what time should one leave home, and into what type of living environment one should enter. However, it is essential that we distinguish the objective of avoiding dependence on *parents*, from the philosophy of withholding trust in, and reliance on, *anyone*. We can consider the extreme: One could have nothing to do with one's parents, and yet still be heavily dependent on someone else. Certain cultures emphasise leaving home as soon as possible as a way of showing initiative, fortitude, determination—a breaking away from an easy but controlled life. Those who do this might then either move in with friends or lovers, or they might just live on their own. Their choice might be out of financial considerations, or it might be that leaning on others in such a situation is not as obvious as depending on parents. When living at home, everyone knows the tendency is to depend on parents, but when living with others, the level of dependency is more private. Compared to living with one's parents, one can be just as much, if not more of a burden, on a friend, lover or spouse.

Hence, the meaningful cultural issue of claiming independence, the way that someone 'announces' their adulthood, is most visible in the act of departing from the household of origin, or as it simply known, 'leaving home'. If this age is too early, then the family appears unkind, if the age is seen as too late, then the individual appears immature and weak. Whatever the emotional consequences, in Western societies such as the United States, Germany, Denmark, Australia, and Britain, the age of leaving home is declining, although such an event is becoming increasingly a move to *independent* living, rather than marriage. In the period from the early 1950s to the late 1960s, the proportion of women leaving home for marriage was only about 50%, and for men about 45%.[27] The more recent developments in home-leaving can be attributed neither to marriage, nor to entry into work, school, parenthood, or military service roles. Many did not leave home despite entry into these roles, and many did leave without entering any of them.[28]

If marriage is not the specific impetus for leaving the family of childhood, why then do people depart? There are three groups that each have their own views about the reasons for leaving home, groups which are most noticeably distinguished by their phase of maturity. The first group are those who leave at around the legal age of majority of 18; the second are those who leave between majority age and mid-20; the third are those who leave as older adults, after their mid-20s.

The members of the first group were in earlier times motivated primarily by *practical* factors, but eventually based their decision to conform to a model emphasising social duty. The demands of home life were eclipsed by the call to adhere to a legalistic definition of 'adult'. Regardless of one's emotional, financial or psychological state, age 18, the 'magic number', became the time to cut loose, to 'individuate' both for the good of the individual and society. Yet the definition of what 'adult' actually means changes according to cultural and situational factors. In most countries, there is a dichotomy between the official majority age of 18, and the 'unofficial' majority age of 21, with no immediately clear rational basis as to why one or the other is used. When it comes to voting, driving a car, military service, sexual license (including marriage), 18 is usually the acceptable age; when it comes to drinking, attending nightclubs, viewing exotic or salacious entertainment, then 21 is the correct adult age. Those activities for which the age of 18 is appropriate revolve around productivity and positive contribution to society, whereas the activities approved for people 21 and over are more often than not superficial. Restriction on the latter activities carries an implicit sense of danger of succumbing to temptation, a weak threat in a society that has already given those under age 21 numerous licences. Having attained many serious responsibilities, the 18-year-old must wonder what unfathomable process takes several years to complete before he can taste the full plate of life's offerings. It is quite apparent that these are contradictory standards, and that there is a good chance that when it comes to the individual assessing his own feeling as to how 'adult' he is, he will be baffled.[29] This group is most likely to be insecure in its notions of independence.

The second group contains members with perhaps mixed intentions, people who do not yet know which model of adult responsibilities should be accepted. They feel that 18 is too young, but 21 might be too old, although the departure by two or three years after the later age is necessary to avoid being considered aberrant by modern standards. These issues are tied into the process of college education. Since most people obtain an associate or bachelor's degree by age 21 or 22, thereby completing their education, the age of 21 would appear the right time to grant the individual full privileges and rights, since they then have full responsibility.

The third group contains individuals who still steadfastly cling to the traditional idea that it is prudent to *stay at home until marriage* or at least until they are well placed enough to establish their own household. Privileges and rights are irrelevant, unless one is certain that one can fully utilise them. They seem to be fairly unconcerned about the 'decent' time to leave home and begin their own adult lives. Many of these might be immigrants or the children of immigrants from more traditional nations, where at the time of their emigration the modernist ethos had not yet found a comfortable dwelling place. Others might simply see the prudence in remaining at home, whilst finishing school, and saving money for marriage. Living at home is certainly the cheapest alternative, for it allows the individual to forego paying rent, food, clothing, and so on (or at least a large portion of these expenses) and instead putting them into savings accounts and investments. Proved by centuries of experience, this is the most rapid way to build a 'dowry' for women, and a capital investment for men.

Strong evidence exists that Western society has experienced a significant decline in the age of leaving the home of childhood, with this phenomenon being propelled by legalistic concepts. In the US in the period 1920-1979, there has been a dramatic drop in the percent of people who remain living with their parents as adults. During the 1950s, the decline was attributable to a drop in the age of marriage, but after this, the rising age in marriage has *not* resulted in a consistent increase in the proportion of adults living with their parents. Subsequent periods saw a consistent reduction in numbers living at home as adults, especially for older individuals. In the 1920-39 period, nearly 30% of males and females were still living at home with parents by age 30. Half of the males and 37% of females age 26 and over were still living at home in this period. The proportions age 26 and over still living at home declined to 20% and 13% respectively by 1965-69.[30]

The reluctance to remain in the family home continued to become more prominent in the industrially advanced nations. In a study by Yi et al. (1994), figures for the United States, France and Sweden point to a major change in concepts of independence in the

West. In the US, the percent of males who were 25 and over when they left home for good was 21% in between 1950 and 1960, but this declined to only 14% by the period 1970-1980; the figures for females was 13% and 8%, respectively. In France, for males it was 38% and 24%, for females it was 32% and 19%, respectively. For Swedes, it was 38% and 15% for males, and 15% to 8% for females, respectively.

We can see that *departing from one's household of origin when well into adulthood has become a minority phenomenon,* no doubt with all the attendant social disapproval that follows any minority action, regardless of the wisdom of that action in relation to one's personal life goals.

To obtain a deeper understanding, we must look at patterns of home-leaving. If there is little outside influence to leave home, then we should see gradual changes in the tendency to leave home over the ages. There would be peaks, but not very strongly defined. We know in this case that there is little outside influence, since we would expect each individual to have myriad factors to determine that age at which he or she would desire to exit the current family situation. It would be highly unlikely that the exigencies of life for most people would all centre around 18 or 21. On the other hand, if there were sharp rises and strong peaks, then we could say there was an *externally* determined force that encouraged people to leave. Using the study mentioned above, we see that for both American males and females in the period 1970-80, compared to other ages, there was a sharp increase in the tendency to leave the family of origin between ages 17 and 18, and this drops off steeply until 21, then the decline is more gradual. It is a similar case for Sweden, although there is a more gradual decline from 19 to 23, then a sharp drop, then after age 26 there is a very gradual decline, similar to that of the United States. The proportion of people departing home in France peaks later than the other two countries at age 21, with a steep rise that begins at age 18. For ages 21 to 26, there is a rapid decline analogous to the one in the US, followed by a much more gradual decline.

It appears, therefore, that externally derived forces are responsible for at least facilitating, if not encouraging home-leaving, producing the concept that every person must execute a 'basic duty' to society by becoming a worker and consumer. The belief that one should leave home only after attaining minimal social competence and skills is not stressed.

Further, this 'appropriate' age appears to have fallen over time. In Sweden, in the period 1960-80, the median age plunged from 24 to 21 for males, yet changed little for women, going from 21 to 20. France experienced a similar decrease in average age for males and females, from age 24 to 22, in the period 1962-1975. For American males and females, the median age for leaving home remained steady at about 20 over the period 1950-1980. Thus, in at least two countries, there was major change in views about leaving home in the period from the 1960s to the 1970s. This change in attitude could not possibly be attributed to young people suddenly developing much greater life skills. Rather, there must have been a cultural modification in these countries that accounts for the lower age of leaving. The only reason for living with parents was to reach *minimal* mental and physical maturity, with other reasons, such as protection and security, becoming largely irrelevant.

How do these factors affect the propensity and desire for marriage? There is no doubt that the attitudes of parents and relatives contribute to the child's development of views concerning independence and family life. Nonetheless, social forces, as well as personal preferences, can also modify these views. Research shows that in general young adults, more than their parents, expect to depart home to live in a separate residence (with others or alone) before marriage. Step-parent families, more than other families, expect children to leave home early and to marry at the 'appropriate' age. In mother-only families, children expect to leave home early only because they want to *delay* marriage. A lower level of closeness in a family, as often seen in non-intact, non-traditional families, appears to precipitate expectations of earlier 'nest-leaving'.[31] This view results because of an inability of parents to organise activities within the household in consonance with their child's personality and temperament. Tensions arise whenever a child feels he or she is not being treated equitably as a result of parenting resources being spread too thin. Consequently, women from large families have a *lower* probability of earlier marriage, and individuals who come from single-parent households are more likely to exit early for independent living, though again *not* for marriage.[32] The latter have formed a negative concept of marriage, both intellectually and as experience, and are eager to leave in order to form their own household. People who come from households where an affectionate family situation is absent, would want to avoid getting involved in marriage themselves—a form of life that seems little more than an offensive or insulting 'condition', and one that should, if possible, be avoided.

When negative factors of home life are felt in the aggregate, a concomitant change in behaviour patterns will occur. These households are characterised by distancing between parents and children, followed by a general breakdown in relations. That there is a disturbing rise in the incidence of these types of dysfunctional households is beyond dispute,[33] and it helps to explain the downward trend in the age of leaving home. Thus, a phenomenon that appears to be based solely on a social rule relating to economic productivity is, in fact, also influenced by a personal desire to leave.

Hence, there are two distinct decisions made in reference to this critical choice of departure. One involves determining the appropriateness of continuing to live at home, the other involves ascertaining the likelihood of obtaining the type of residence and social situation that is harmonious with one's personality and goals. Certain environmental factors are involved in these decisions. For example, relatively high national, but not necessarily local, unemployment and lower population density *decrease* the probability of women departing for marriage or independent living. In addition, if the head of the household has a college degree, leaving for women, but not men, is less likely.[34] It is apparent that those women living in less crowded areas, at a time when unemployment nationally is high, and where parents are well-educated, will find it less prudent to leave home. If presented with the choice of living with parents or living alone or with someone else, the individual might choose to simply remain at home if job opportunities are poor, outside social interactions are irregular, and parents can act as friends and respected authority figures, relatively enlightened and competent in attitudes and behaviours.

The second decision includes a number of alternatives that must be scrutinised: One can depart to live alone with one other person, with several other persons, or with a spouse. The choice of new living arrangement is a function of one's attitudes and one's income; to this extent, it is a more complicated matter than considering the suitability of continuing to live with parents. Underlying the decision to live alone or with someone else are one's attitudes towards one's role in marriage and how this role will 'play out' within a particular social context. We can see, therefore, that the creation of a living arrangement is based as much on privately derived marriage intentions, as on economic, material, and cultural factors.

Let us now assume that the individual has decided to leave home, and is going through various steps to create an environment that he or she finds conducive. The following table shows how the factors we have been discussing—gender, income, and orientation to marriage—influence a person's decision either to live with an unrelated individual, or to live alone:[35]

Table 1.

LIVING SITUATION AS RELATED TO SEX, INCOME, AND SOCIAL ORIENTATION

	Income level high	Income level low
Females	with others[L]/marry later[L]	alone[C,L]/marry earlier[C]
Males	alone[L]/marry earlier[C]	with others[C,L]/marry later[C,L]

C - Conservative in social orientation, L - Liberal in social orientation

We can see that this decision to live alone or with others also has a bearing on marriage propensity. Thus, women with higher incomes tend to live with someone but marry *later*, whilst males with higher income tend to live alone but marry *earlier*. Clearly, men and women have two *different* dynamics in operation in their choice of lifestyle. At base, *the large majority of each sex desires some level of companionship by living with people of similar backgrounds, which would include age, class, education and, perhaps most importantly, income*.[36] But there is also a segment of each population that for innate reasons (temperament) desires independence, possibly *in association with some kind of steady companionship*. These desires are influenced to a large extent by financial factors.

However, orientation towards marriage has its own effects. Having high income, conservative men can almost immediately realise their marriage goals (if a woman is willing to wed), and liberal men can immediately realise their goal of being independent by acquiring their own residence. Men of conservative orientation might have the same needs as women for intimate friendship, but being the traditional providers for the family, they would desire *both* to bring in abundance as well as obtain companionship. For a time these men might live alone, when economic conditions permit, in order to show that they can achieve the independence ethos. With lower income, those men who foresee marriage at some point must almost certainly live with others with the purpose

of conserving funds; those men who want to be perpetually independent must delay their independence and *also* live with others
until they too have adequate savings. In this category, the independent group is 'swallowed up' and is no longer noticeable by
itself the way it was in the high income category (the ones who live
alone). Men who both love autonomy and those who hate it might
very well be sharing lodgings with at least the same short term
goal: To save money.

The conservative woman might wish to marry early when she
is not earning much money, and the liberal woman might live
alone out of a strong desire for independence. In addition, there
might be some conservative women who for a time will live alone
as well, out of a desire to achieve a modicum of independence.
Women might feel that they do not need to save as much money
as men since the latter are the traditional economic providers and
would probably take the lead in savings. This would explain why
women with lower incomes might not have a need to save money
by sharing a residence.

Why would women share a residence, and defer marriage when
earning a *higher* income? One reason might be that women who
have high-paying, and thus career-demanding lives, are more likely
to have greater difficulty making sacrifices in marriage relationships. We have already mentioned the difficulties caused by the
'importing' of stress into the household from the office. Perhaps
possessing and/or wanting to maintain higher ideals about marriage, women might see this kind of friction as the major contribut-
ing factor to the alarmingly high divorce rates; they wonder
whether they themselves will ever be secure in a marriage. The
need for balance then becomes important (as was discussed on
page 4). The satisfactory maintenance of the two different spheres
of work and home is perceived as taxing intellectual and emotional
resources. As a result, career women set up their lives in such a
way, so that conflict in either sphere can be met with routes that

afford protection and escape. If a woman is earning a low income, living with a man whom she feels might eventually withdraw his affections would make her dependent and vulnerable, whereas living by herself gives her more control over her destiny. A low income often means few savings and few alternatives; conflict in this 'marriage' would entail meagre choices for such a woman, who does not have the money to relocate elsewhere, at least not in the near future. On the other hand, if she is earning a high income, then she might cohabit with a man, forming a close approximation of a marital relationship, in the knowledge that it can be broken off relatively easily. Her 'partner' will have less of an opportunity to exploit her, as the woman has enough resources to keep her own life secure. She is not dependent on a man for her residence, her possessions, or her livelihood; her only weakness is her emotional dependence, something far more difficult to remedy than any material circumstance.

If a woman with a complex but financially rewarding occupation often experiences problems with relationships, and if she can live comfortably on her own income, then why not avoid these problems of companionship altogether by living alone? Why does our table above show a tendency to live with others? We may posit that women in these positions are lonely and insecure and desire companionship as compensation. This insecurity might not stem from the rigours of the job itself, but from her social position. A woman with a good salary clearly has power and prerogatives that a poorer woman does not. However, the benefits of such propitious remuneration create problems on their own. Women earning a high income is definitely unusual by traditional standards, and this group might largely be populated by individuals who are not interested in such standards, that is, persons who consider themselves social liberals. Therefore, whereas it was not unusual in the past to see both high- and low-earning men, it was highly exceptional to come across high-earning women.

Thus, well-paid women are likely to see themselves even today as belonging to a different social category from other women, being viewed as 'contemporary', 'modern', or 'fashionable' by virtue of an external factor, namely, their *occupation* alone. Perhaps because of this, women may be more *model conscious* than men, understanding the world in terms of explicit 'right' and 'wrong' life courses and using moral factors more readily when making major decisions. Women, desiring independence and privacy as much or more than men, evidently can use the companionship of a *roommate as a proxy for that of a husband's*. Especially if a career-orientated woman is liberal in her social views, a possibility to which we alluded earlier, she might feel she is 'not the marrying type', but still live with someone anyway. She utilises an external factor in her favour in this case; a woman who cohabits with a man might use, as a shield against community criticism, the respectability gained from higher occupational status. In these situations, women would obviously place more emphasis on income as a status marker. To look at this another way, a woman with a low income would be marked as 'traditional', even if she is not actually so, and she might avoid sharing a residence with a man, especially in a sexual relationship. Women who have lower status occupations could not, in a modern context, use their status as protection from communal and family criticism. They would be more likely to view marriage as the only respectable context of a physically intimate relationship.

Overall, we find that the departure from home involves both cultural and personal influences. There are those who, because of their temperament, wish to leave home by age 18, others because they feel that the community expects them to do so, others because they do not feel comfortable with life at home, and yet others because they are attracted to the advantages of the independent life. It is interesting to note that *conservative values still hold sway in a modern society that has ostensibly 'liberated' itself from them;*

whatever his personal beliefs, every individual has to, sooner or later, confront these traditional concepts. Some are trying to implement these traditional values, whilst others are reacting against them. Those who wish to save money could marry as soon as possible, and form a considerate, cooperative relationship; they could be called conservative. Those who cultivate their independence in pursuit of a 'light-hearted', gregarious life, with a practicable escape route from misfortunate emotional relationships, could justifiably be called liberals.

Earlier we discerned a cultural continuity in attitudes when studying the effect of economic factors on marital dynamics. Here, we see many men and women also follow traditional European concepts when it comes to their *desire for companionship* after leaving their household of origin. Nonetheless, desires are always affected by other factors, some of which are not within the control of the individual. The important life event of 'leaving home' is now dependent on a standardised/idealised dynamic of home life, namely, one that integrates how one should associate with parents, siblings, neighbours, and peers. As such, this event is now often a function of external, and not necessarily advantageous, forces. Such a situation not only produces a threat to the future, but also engenders a disturbing picture of the present, when social demands, some quite intangible, begin to contaminate a decision that will profoundly affect the individual's relationships and social competence for possibly many years. We concluded previously (page 33) that in the modern industrial materialist society, marital prospects and conjugal happiness rest precariously on difficult-to-obtain accomplishments in education and career. If the person is struggling to live without support, on his own, before he has developed appropriate competence, his relationships might waver in purpose and intent. We could say that the 'container' of marriage might then genuinely be uncomfortable in experience, as well as unconformable to expectations.

Nevertheless, this is not exclusively a phenomenon of the modern age, for our ancestors might in some cases have also been reacting to the quality of their family life in their decision to marry. In any case, the importance of building a mature personality, as well as adequate financial resources, in preparation for marriage cannot be overemphasised.

How the individual begins his adult life often determines how well he will live it; we could say: *Limit the growth of resources early on, and you reduce the range of choices you have in a marriage partner, timing of marriage, and lifestyle.* This tendency to leave home early, when not solely based on thorough objective evaluation of the facts, can imperil the welfare not only of one person, but of a whole family.

In this chapter, we have studied the phenomenon of building of perceptions of maturity occur in Western society. The 'marker' of leaving the household of childhood is a very great one, but there is another 'marker', that of the new 'independent' household, that also signifies aspects of one's social competence. We have seen how income, gender, and orientation to marriage interact to influence the decisions relating to living arrangement after leaving the home of childhood. It is, however, this *orientation to marriage*, i.e. the personal attitudes towards companionship, that are rarely discussed, and so are poorly understood. Let us now look more closely at this factor, and in particular, let us examine how this interacts with economic factors that might help or hinder realising personal goals.

Chapter 5

Living Arrangements and the Propensity to Marry

*A*vowals of autonomy, which are clear and unequivocal, are not common, but one could easily assume 'leaving home' is a firm personal statement about one's confidence in the ability to tackle any and all of life's problems without the protection, support, or safety net of parents. Nevertheless, the evidence from Western societies shows that young people are not quite saying this; they often try to attain *both* standards of independence and dependence. A person might have a strong orientation towards marriage, but at the same time, he might still desire the freedom to carry out his intentions without interference from a spouse. Of course, everyone would like the freedom to choose friends and residence, with a 'backup' of mother and father's resources when required; some people desire more support than others, and some people desire to be left alone. Realistically, though, economic factors might have a major influence in determining the household type a person enters after leaving the home of childhood. Notwithstanding the type of living arrangement that a person will eventually settle upon in a new household, there will always be an innate preference for a certain configuration. Clearly, a number of factors affect the decision to leave home, and a number of factors affect the kind of household one would prefer to set up.

Therefore, what are the personal motivations for leaving the household of origin and moving in with someone else? It is entirely probable that one or both partners have at least some significant dislike of living with their families. They might not get along because parents are overly demanding or critical, children might be obstreperous. Moving in with someone else is an escape that gives the individual a freedom to do what he or she pleases, things that they could not do at home. Further, life at home might be cramped, uncomfortable, and unstable. Such vicissitudes might be elemental in forming the dream of a new life on one's own, where one has privacy and latitude in behaviour. Indeed, it might be a form of emancipation, of being set free from familial 'bondage', and for some it cannot come too soon. It would be short-sighted to suggest, however, that such individuals want to be all *alone*; they wish companionship, but on different terms. And so moving out from the family household undoubtedly relates, though indirectly, to the subject of marriage and cohabitation.

On the other hand, those who have no great love of familial 'emancipation' are characterised by certain factors as well. Women, and especially men, who live with parents well into adulthood (i.e., someone over age 30 who never left home, or who left and then returned) are different in personality and temperament compared to those who left at the average age. These individuals tend to be disproportionately widowed, separated, or divorced, of lower education, and not in the labour force. If they are working, they might have average incomes, but are still less likely to have attended college. Many persons who are still living with parents at a later age can be characterised as having less capability of independent living, having a lower capacity for work, and having an inability to attain better paying jobs; males in this situation could, in particular, be unmarriageable.[37] Some return home after divorce, or unemployment in order to regain confidence, and then they remarry or get another job, leaving home once again. Others might become permanent dependents because of mental or physical disability. In a certain sense, this conforms to traditional patterns, of men and women who have become comfortable with living at home, of parents who liked having one child live with them, and of children who never much liked competitive positions, work, or education. In this way, the household of origin provides a life-long refuge, and if recognised as such, and legitimated by society, individuals would not necessarily feel the need to move out from their parents' abode if they felt more comfortable living there. It is evident that as long as people incorporate into their lives the empowering essence of traditional moral principles, they should not be forced to become something they are not. The conflict in modern society could theoretically be lowered, if people established a lifestyle that is more in keeping with their personalities. If individuals are inclined to develop a *companionate* relationship *external* to the family, and this is by no means a universal need, a delay in leaving home might give them more time to find someone of compatible temperament and personality, and their ideal of love might substantively be reached.

By studying the *nature and succession of living arrangements* a person procures in early life, we might be able to understand that person's concept of companionship, and what this person really desires in relationships. Across the Western world, a pattern indeed emerges when comparing the tendency to marry early or late with the individual's residential status in early adulthood. Those unmarried persons who were *living alone* at the average age of 21 had the clearest relationship to marriage inclination, with the propensity to *marry late*.[38] *Living at home at an early age increases* the likelihood of marrying *early*, and conversely lowers the chance of marrying late.[39] Further, *those who lived with friends, acquaintances or roommates were more likely to marry early*.[40] Women who are moderately to strongly 'marriage-avoidant' (percent not married by age of 45 as well as those marrying at 30 or above) tend *not* to have lived with parents or other family members in early adulthood.[41] Goldscheider & Waite (1987), in an American study, found that living independently *delays* marriage, especially for younger adults and women, although it is less of an influence when living with others, as in group quarters.

The information above can be condensed into a table, where the increasing desire for independence or autonomy is seen going from top to bottom, and left to right (figures in parentheses indicate statistical significance not reached):

Table 2.

PROPENSITY TO MARRY AS A FUNCTION OF RESIDENCE STATUS AT AGE 21

	Marry 19 and under, males & females	Marry 19 and under, males	Marry 30 and over, females	Marry 30 and over, males	Not married by age 45, females
Living with parents	+			-	(-)
Living with family			(-)	(-)	(-)
Living with friends	+	+			(-)
Living alone	-		+	+	(+)

We see in this analysis the existence of two population segments, one that greatly desires *freedom and independence*, and who are most likely to be seen living alone in apartments or other residence and marrying late; the other segment greatly desires *companionship*, if not at home then with friends as roommates, with a concomitant tendency to marry earlier. The former might become bachelors of long standing, clearly independent-minded, who are often characterised as being 'set in their ways'. They like peace, quiet, having things in life arranged to their taste and expectations; they would detest the disruption brought on by the activities of a wife and children. For the latter, they like to live with others, and are willing to leave the parental abode, but do not wish to live alone. They then live with one or more other persons, and then also tend to marry at some point in their lives. Wishing to achieve some kind of 'in-between' compromise situation, they were not so intent on living independently, but yet could not continue residing with their parents.

Thus, the decision to leave one's home of origin is usually predicated on a number of considerations. One has to ask oneself a number of questions. Am I happy living with my parents and siblings? Would I be happier living by myself, or with someone else? Could I support myself and still save money when living on my own? Would I be secure and content living alone, perhaps for many years? In spite of this social network one might construct, living by oneself does not meet the needs of intimacy, and residing in a city creates an even greater distance between oneself and the social environment. The negative psychological effects that arise from these deficiencies during adverse and stressful periods might be serious.[42] But many would rather face this prospect than endure perhaps even more serious problems living at home with dysfunctional parents and siblings, where solutions to one's problems might be almost entirely outside of one's grasp. Clearly, in most cases there are factors that push people out the door and pull them to a new situation; it is very easy to confuse the two. When one decides to marry or move in with someone else, the ostensible reason might be that one has fallen in love with that person, although the 'love' that one speaks of, is a love of the *freedom that awaits in a new living situation*.

Because of this emphasis on the 'new living situation' possibly without adequately analysing the material aspects, we should examine the basic nature of housing and how people deal with it as a factor in life.

Out of a desire for privacy or seclusion comes the requirement for physical space, and housing is therefore a fundamental factor in human existence. The critical need for openness around one's person is intrinsic to all people, and indeed even other mammals. Not surprisingly, a serious unsolicited intrusion into one's space can be taken as a threat of violence, with a preemptive attack as justified. These desires vary according to culture, with European, especially Western European, cultures requiring more privacy than others. The type of family structure commonly seen in our history, that is, the nuclear household, and the kind of physical partitioning commonly seen in better homes, demonstrate a deep-seated requirement for retreat and seclusion, by oneself or with a loved one. One must be able to have quiet for rest or reflection, and a freedom to live out one's vocation or avocations without interruption or encroachment.

We know that the availability of housing, of private space, is a crucial factor in determining the appropriateness of marriage, as we saw earlier in relation to Madrid (page 11). Housing costs are a critical yet underrated factor, ignored by citizen and social planner alike. The first domain supplies a crucial initial context of marriage, for it is the physical space in which intellectual and emotional development will occur. Evidence exists for the deleterious effects of residential living space shortages and how much space is allotted to each partner can often have significant consequences. Although psychological well-being is not necessarily an effect of crowding, it often does result in lower marital well-being.[43] Marital happiness is a function of factors related to the couple's dwelling, which makes it imperative that housing is acceptable since it threatens the marriage directly. However, the acceptability of the situation is not immediately obvious, since a subjective assessment of adequacy of space is a better predictor of satisfaction than an objective assessment. Cooperation and elucidation of standards are critical to companionate relationships.

Thus, to wed or cohabit without surveying the housing market first is careless to say the least, as the relationship between husband and wife can be severely strained if space requirements are not met. An appropriate strategy would be to assess one's housing preferences, to assess the housing situation, and then to make suitable plans for how much of the household income is to be used in this fashion. As with any item in the budget, it must be evaluated in light of the constraints imposed by other items. Therefore, a couple's requirements about the 'proper residence', in terms of accessibility, size, conveniences, age of structure, and aesthetic considerations, must be reconciled with their plans for schooling, employment, children, possessions and savings.

Marriages are weakest when external factors dictate compromise in key areas. Such a feeling arises when prices of residences rise more rapidly than income, as then high prices mean high mortgage payments or high rents. During a critical period of social change in America, single family, apartment, condominium, and cooperative prices had all risen to levels that make housing expenses difficult to support in a middle-class budget. Between 1970 and 1987, personal income per capita in the United States increased from $4,056 to $15,495 (3.8x),[44] yet the average new privately owned one family house (the 'ideal' for most people) price rose from $23,400 to $104,500, a four-and-a-half fold increase,[45] but existing house prices rose somewhat in tandem with income, from $23,000 to $85,600 (3.7x). The magnitude of change was greater than the national average in the Northeast (5.3x), and in the West (4.7x), but was lower than average in the Midwest (3.3x).[46] Hence, prices of new houses, and, in certain regions of the country older houses, outstripped the growth of personal income, causing an increase in the size of this item in the household budget. In addition, in certain regions of the country, the growth in house prices was far more than the increase in income, a fact not expressed in the above statistics. This important trend shows little sign of abating, even now in the 21st century. This situation would clearly put a damper on the exercise of personal concepts of privacy and autonomy.

Many other countries, including the United Kingdom, Germany, Australia, Belgium, Denmark and Sweden suffer from high housing costs, but this exorbitance might apply to different *types* of housing. For example, in one nation, rental units are very expensive, and in another, smaller 'starter' houses are difficult to obtain, and yet in another, larger 'trade-up' family type houses are costly. Still, this situation is preferable to ones where housing, of certain types, is virtually unavailable at any price. During the era of Communist regimes in Eastern Europe, housing, like other markets, was centrally controlled so that prices were kept within the range of affordability; the problem was availability. Often the situation was so bleak that the only residence a young couple could afford during their early years was an apartment that was shared with one or other set of parents. Ironically, they considered the death of a relative as one of the only opportunities to gain control of their own household. Many couples might not be so fortunate, and have to spend their entire married lives in the same household, essentially moving to their parent's bedroom once they die, and then having their own children and their spouses live with them, repeating the cycle once again.

We should point out, though, that the desire to live with relations might be more a function of culture than finances. In the mid-20th century United States, married couples of Russian origin were inclined more than other groups to have elderly parents living with them, whereas Italian-Americans tended to have married children living in their homes, but German-Americans were least likely to have either older or younger relatives living with them.[47] These ethnic groups were not very different from each other in average income, occupations, or social class, and so differences in living arrangements can probably be attributed to temperamental factors. Germans might very well have a more independent or autonomous persona than Italians or Russians, a disposition which would affect their housing requirements. Thus, if temperamental factors were allowed to flourish, instead of being overawed by 'Anglo-Saxon' ideas, then there would be less pressure on housing in America, and the economy could be organised in such a way that housing was made affordable.[48]

When someone is unable to immediately buy or rent what he or she considers a sufficiently large residence, patiently waiting for such an opportunity can be difficult when holding in abeyance other considerations. Fulfilling goals relating to housing is often viewed as vitiating both the independence ethos and marriage ethos. Various methods might be pursued to find housing quickly, such as working longer hours, changing jobs, borrowing or even misappropriation. Accordingly, the proportion of the family budget that is made up by housing expenses is an influence that increases or decreases marriage age, as higher income and greater savings are necessary before a couple can live comfortably. In many cases where people marry young, they must live with the husband or wife's parents for a time until circumstances improve. In most Western cultures, this is considered undesirable as the couple expects privacy and control over the affairs of their household.[49] We can see that, as the costs related to housing ascend as a percent of a household budget, the *less* the chance of a woman marrying young.[50] The option of living with one's spouse, as well as with relatives and/or in a small residence, is generally less attractive than living on one's own, or with a roommate, other things being the same.

Instead of the availability of housing determining marriage age, there is an alternative model we might consider: Lower housing costs are associated with lower age of marriage, because younger married couples spend *less* on housing. Young couples have fewer resources, and so they cannot spend much on housing, instead preferring to concentrate on other expense areas, including clothing, entertainment, food, and transportation. It is questionable, however, whether these couples have much control over the housing expense item in their budget. The choice of housing is often the product of location and cultural pressure to attain an appropriate status. How can people of middle class and upper class backgrounds choose smaller units, with inferior amenities, perhaps in poorer neighbourhoods, without experiencing some kind of disapproval from colleagues and friends? Hence, the scaling of costs relating to housing and rentals is determined by a variety of factors, economic and social, whereas other portions of a household budget are more amenable to a couple's control than housing. A couple's greatest asset in this regard is the ability to migrate to an area with housing on a different scale, yet this is difficult to accomplish when the character, location and features of one's residence currently confer a certain prestige.

The reality is that individuals must find some kind of balance between their spatial needs, their emotional desires, their income, and housing costs. We have discussed in this chapter the ways in which people attempt to approach this problem, and have found that whilst people still depend on one another, and there is no monolithic need for total freedom (i.e., solitary living), *external factors still give people less freedom in their choice of living arrangement than they would like.* Once again, we see that a complex mix of economic, psychological, cultural, and temperamental ingredients determine the dimensions of companionship in which a person must live out his life. The individual must be prudent, intelligent, cautious, and, most of all, courageous, in how he assesses and arranges the resources he has at his disposal.

We have in previous sections discovered how the factors of social competence and materialism impact living arrangements, but in this chapter we discovered that an unexpectedly strong factor in decision-making was the *concept of independence*. Although we have realised that this concept is a force in most individuals, it was not apparent that the 'independence ethos' goes beyond the desire to win challenges without major support from others; we now see that it entails removing even *stages of minor support* on a routine level, producing an actual *physical separation* within the social environment. Let us now examine more closely how this dynamic has formed, and what consequences it can have, by extending our analysis of how the needs of *autonomy* and *privacy* can influence the propensity for marriage, and configuration of living arrangements. Indeed, these needs might very well be overriding in importance. We have learned that cultural factors can have a surprisingly strong effect on how people deal with the housing situation in their community, so we should endeavour to examine in greater detail how a person's concept of *autonomy*, interacts with his or her need for *privacy, within* the confines of a residence, keeping in mind that both are significantly affected by external mechanisms.

Chapter 6

Concepts of
Space and Privacy

*W*hile the goal of obtaining a residence after leaving the home of origin appears to be relatively simple, there are various issues that must be resolved, the most significant of which is residence size, or amount of living space. On a simple level, the average individual assesses the potential for housing using experiences gained from his own circumstances. In general, a person who grew up in a household where living space was small will expect difficulties in relocating to a large residence of his own. On the other hand, a person whose childhood was spent in a home where there was more than adequate space might believe that finding a large house for himself will be easy. If a man determines the space available to average person in his country, he is not only establishing the probable parameters of his future residence, but also his capacity for finding private residential space of an expected size.

There are, however, more complex factors which alter the *perceptions* of personal living space. Space can be seen as functioning at two levels, at the level of *fundamental need*, and at the level of *status marker*. At its most basic, the desire for space is intrinsic for good mental and physical health, for overcrowding brings disease and psychological problems, and so there is no doubt that humans instinctually desire more living space. Further, in all societies, living apart is a symbol of power. Since having space is an advantage in every culture, the more space one has, the higher one's social status. As a result, a superfluity of space might bring respect and admiration from others, but is also might generate haughtiness and arrogance in the person who benefits from that space.

The concept that large living space brings about status is clearly related to the desire for individualism. Let us examine this more closely. The super-concept of individuality holds an undeniably noble place in European culture, and is responsible for bestowing on Europe and the world almost innumerable innovations, inventions, creations, and designs that have produced immense benefit. Yet, this super-concept is not discussed frequently in the media or in private settings. Possibly because of its virtual 'sacredness', the super-concept is removed from ordinary discourse, lest someone 'profane' something that is so important to such a large portion of the human race. Instead, derived concepts, which are safer, are more likely to be addressed. Two of these derivations are privacy and autonomy, which as modern 'representatives' of the super-concept, are promoted by all schools and media institutions.

Based on simple observation of social trends over the last century, one can see that the two social forces that most powerfully affect opinions—schooling (obtaining academic qualifications through attendance at recognised scholastic institutions), and media (institutions that produce information through broadcasting)—combine to form a person's true 'education'. Moreover, higher levels of *education* means getting a higher 'dose' of the concepts of privacy and independence. Both school and media can be said to create an 'information culture', which has a critical effect on how privacy and independence are perceived.

Consequently, abstract concepts related to individuality become very real and tangible when the issue of living space is under consideration. Further, these abstract concepts—personal freedom, privacy, and status—must mediate, or modify, the individual's responses to his present and future living situation (alone or with others). Thus, the *propagation* of these factors through various institutions can alter attitudes on marriage, possibly in a way contrary to the individual's own personal ideals. We hypothesise that better-educated and better-informed people believe that independence and privacy are primary matters, and they see leaving a small household of origin residence as a short-term solution, offering an escape from a difficult situation. The less-educated and informed group puts such matters further down on the list, as they seek longer-term solutions, and wish to conserve resources by staying at home and not moving out. Hence, we can put forward two models, each one based on the level of education.

In the 'less education' scenario, the individual must forbear, and wait for adequate space to become available; even though he might not like living at home with his family in small or cramped quarters, he knows he stands a good chance of eventually finding better accommodations. *His worldview values privacy, but not necessarily leisure or independence.* By living at home in small quarters he loses privacy, but will hopefully gain it later, and in doing this he does not feel he has violated a major social ethic. Living in larger quarters means he has a better chance of attaining privacy in the household of origin, than in some other household, his own or sharing it with someone. Moreover, this abundance then means more space is available elsewhere, *ceteris paribus*, and so he will feel more confident seeking a spouse.

The 'more education' model finds the individual wishing to move out of a smaller home environment into one more fitting his preferences. He has based his worldview on certain relatively unalterable premises, specifically that *independence, privacy, and leisure are essential for a successful life*. It is, however, very difficult to achieve all three simultaneously, as most living arrangements involve sacrificing at least one. Living at home in smaller quarters denies him independence and privacy, but allows him leisure; living alone or with someone else in a smaller residence, whilst working to support himself, denies him leisure and privacy, but allows him greater independence; living at home in larger quarters gives him privacy and ease, but he lacks independence. The third situation would be the one most preferable, until the desire for true autonomy becomes overwhelming.

As representative of certain types of thinking and behavioural patterns found in Western cultures, these models assist us in visualise the waves of social influence that have 'washed over' the individual during the course of his life. Let us now see whether these models are correct, and investigate in greater detail the well-established systems that produce the underlying ideas, and the attitude-modifying processes which are triggered by them.

First, we will define the concept of personal or living space. Personal space is specifically the floor space in a residence on which a person can use for his own purposes, be it for walking, sleeping, exercising, storage, and so on. Space might or might not be for one's exclusive use, as it might be part of one's room, or it might be a shared area. Furthermore, the space might be walled in, or some other divider, permanent or temporary, might be emplaced to create privacy. Because of the psychological importance of spreading out one's domain, the greater amount of space available, of whatever type, for one's private use, the greater the amount of 'living space' or 'personal space', and the greater the satisfaction. Indicators of personal space do not always conform to a priori assumptions. We find that in European nations, persons per room is not correlated with square metres per person or with other indicators. Nevertheless, square metres per person is significantly correlated with various indicators, as we shall see below. From this we can determine that not having one's own *room* is of less significance compared to the *size* of one's personal space. The indicator of persons per dwelling is negatively but non-significantly correlated to square metres per person, a weakness that is also surprising, since one would assume that with relatively few exceptions, the more persons per house, the less space each person would have. Evidently, house size and persons per unit fluctuate separately.

The living environment of the household of origin inspires a view of oneself vis-à-vis others, which is often not in relation to any specific individual, but is an overarching theme about social relations. One's house or room, bigger than that of others, is a sign of affluence and independence; this is especially true if one can have a room to oneself, while others of the same social class must share. However, this can only function as such if it is agreed upon in a larger social context as being a *marker* of status. In other more traditional nations, where academics and mass media are not as important, living space, although it does confer some status, is not a major determinant of power and reinforcer of preeminence, as the individual has other, more socially constructive ways, of obtaining respect. The educated person has these ways available to him as well, but they are inadequate in filling his need for differentiation brought about by the intense competition, not only with actual persons, but with myriad 'virtual' peers who can materialise through the various organs of the media.

We recognise that cultural forces can influence ideas about privacy and independence, and these forces can be described as *vectors*, which adjust a person's views and sentiments on the issue of living space. These vectors are visible in two major, consistent, internationally prevalent indicators:

(1) the level of mass communications
(2) the level of schooling

People strive for social differentiation in reaction to what they see and hear in the media. A greater level of communication, by definition, reveals more than the individual knew previously about the behaviour, attitudes and mores of others; this provides the information necessary for individuation. A greater level of schooling also gives individuals more information on how others live. By schooling, we are not only talking about the highest level reached in formal institutional education, but rather its quality and breadth, and the extent to which the desire for knowledge is met, such as can be measured by pupils per teacher and frequency of loans of library books. Due to the strong force of the individuality super-concept, persons with extended, or more intensive, education tend to infuse an idealism about the need for space into their worldview, seeing it in philosophical terms, not merely pragmatic ones. These requirements, coupled with an inclination for 'aristocratic' separate-ness, institute a collective demand for an above average amount of personal space, that is, society fosters an economic programme of building relatively large residential structures. Most importantly, key ideas about autonomy are given by education which alter the purpose of this space, for the emphasis narrows from two or more people to basically only one, the individual.

Thus, a higher level of education, as measured by proxies, pro-duces higher intellectual requirements, which in turn produces an increased need for privacy, study, reading, etc. Overall, concen-trated education produces quite a different perspective on living arrangements, compared to that produced by a more restricted schooling experience.

Of course, within this general scenario there are variations, especially related to social class, and so we must be more specific about what we mean by 'information flow'. The conventional means of 'broadcasting' ideas in a modern Western society is through various diverse means including teachers, newspapers, television, books, magazines, films, plays and radio.[51] Generally, higher news circulation, fewer students per teacher, more loans from the library, and fewer persons per television signify increasing circulation of information. Furthermore, the variables of persons per television set and borrowing library books can act as proxies for higher learning. News circulation is correlated in the opposite direction one would expect, with fewer persons reading newspa-pers being related to a higher prevalence of tertiary level education. This does not mean that educated people obtain less information than others, it might mean that they obtain it from sources other than newspapers, such as magazines, television, radio and libraries, where they might use an 'all-in-one' reference containing current events, entertainment and commentary. Moreover, it is possible that those who are educated, and presumably versed in the ways of academia, will prefer sources that are less-biassed. The frequently partisan or sensational reportage by certain segments of the media can make finding objective information difficult. They may still read certain newspapers of better reputation, but might read them more infrequently than less-educated individuals.

There is little question, however, that people with higher level academic achievement have a greater exposure to various media, which contain references directly, or indirectly, to the *issue of autonomy*. Many regularly gather news stories from certain sources, and it is clear that the wealthy do so far more often than the working and lower classes.[52] Certainly, for the better off, there is a greater interest in the broadcast word, sound and picture.

We can see that this is verified by the data on media usage. Generally speaking, families of diverse income levels do not apportion their funds very differently from one another among expense categories, as in the amounts spent (as a percent of total expenditures) on housing, transportation, apparel, health care, and other expenditures,[53] or on entertainment and reading.[54] But there is a great contrast in how socioeconomic categories allocate their resources (time and money) *among certain specific forms of art and media*. Analysing the situation of the 1980s, a time of major changes in the concepts of autonomy, privacy and marriage, we find evidence of such discrepancies. Of those with incomes under $5000 in 1985, less than 10% saw jazz performances, classical music, opera, musical plays, plays, ballet performances; fewer than 20% visited a museum or art gallery, and only 44% read a novel, short story, poetry or play. There are not many differences between the lowest category and those making $15,000-25,000. Above a household income of $25,000, however, there is a major departure in spending. Whereas of those making $15-$25,000, only 12% saw musical plays, of those making $25-$50,000, 22% did, and of those making over $50,000, 37% did. Of the first category, 9% saw plays, of the second, 14% did, and of the third, 28% did. Less difference is found in the reading of novels, essays, or works of fiction: 53% of the first category read one, 63% of the level above it, and 77% of the highest income level. Perhaps most significantly, because of the cultural importance of the medium, we find that only 19% of the first category visited an exposition of art and culture, such as a gallery or museum in the previous year, as opposed to 28% of the second and an impressive 45% of the third.[55] Finally, those making over $40,000 spent on average nearly $700 for television, radio and sound equipment, compared to only about $290 for those in the $15-19,999 bracket.[56]

A similar dynamic prevails for differences in academic qualifications, as, for example, 80% of those who have graduate school education read a work of fiction in the last year, as opposed to only 52% of high-school graduates.[57] Those who have a graduate school education see musical plays, jazz performances, or visit museums or art galleries at least *three* times more frequently than those with only high school education. The ratio between the two groups rises to at least six to one when the media are classical music, opera, plays, or ballet performances.[58] Clearly, *there is far more exposure to ideas, whether academic, fictional, or historical, when income and educational categories are above middle-range.*

Hence, these findings further verify the correctness of the two models that we posited earlier. All of this leads us to now address this question: How do ideas about living space affect the desire for marriage? In an analysis of Western nations, we see that age of marriage, and so the imputed value of marriage, is indeed affected by the amount of residential space available. The tendency to remain permanently single is affected by space parameters, with more space per person *reducing* the proportion of women who never marry. However, we can refine this further by noting that the influence also varies by *level of education*: For well-educated males and females, *more space* means *later* marriage, and fewer not marrying; for only moderately-educated males and females, *more space* means *earlier* marriage. We should add that, in general, greater use of information in a nation is also associated with having more personal space.[59]

Moreover, the ideas propagated by institutional instruction and mass communication cause financial resources, where available, to be directed toward construction in order to *increase living space*, but when education is not as effective, then funds are used for other purposes. Per capita income shows a correlation with space only when controls are used, it being positively correlated when the ratio of students per teacher is below average, and the ratio of persons per television is also below average (i.e. better schooling and communications). More frequent and broad use of information tends to increase the amount of space available by 'encouraging' a higher standard of living. These findings also support the two models we established earlier. Thus, education influences how space is perceived, and by extension, affects the valuation of marriage and its potential benefits.

Now that we have seen how media and education can affect views of marriage, let us now look at what some may consider the opposite, the effect that flow of information has on ideas about *independence*, since this concept also affects the value of marriage. Indeed, the desire for independence can potentially interfere with the desire for marriage, and the process of attaining it. Marriage in all cultures demands acquiescence to certain conventions, and there is evidence that it might not be possible, in the modern context, for a person to feel 'independent' and be married at the same time.

Research into the social thinking in the Western world indicates that the vectors mentioned above—newspapers, books, college education, television, and teachers—have a major role in affecting attitudes and opinions about satisfaction with home life, groups, work practises, earnings/money issues, social rank, and the general welfare of the nation.[60] Each of the vectors uses audience dependent mechanisms to describe and analyse society, and so each has a different level of depth and scope. We can list in order of approximately *increasing* scope and depth: Television, newspapers, books, high school, college.

We should bear in mind that what is being analysed are *attitudes or opinions, not actual structural or economic changes*. Hence, in a situation of increasing optimism, people might not necessarily be reacting to the actual benefits of a good economy, but to the *perception* that such an economy is present, or will happen in the near future. Similarly, people might perceive that their society is less rank- or status-orientated because its people are well-educated, or they possess easy access to information. Theoretically, it is possible that in a well-educated society, rank is no longer relevant as people become more autonomous, and go beyond a previous ceiling of ability; but the problem lies in belief, as the ideal is not a reality. In fact, our own study shows there is an absence of strong correlations between social division (as measured by percent of total national income earned by households comprising the highest 10% of wage earners) and other indicators: There is no significant correlation with student/teacher ratio; a very weak positive correlation with over 25 with college education ($r=.1888$); a somewhat stronger correlation with persons per television ($r=.3920$); and a negative correlation with library loans of books ($r=-.3018$).

Thus, in a developing economy, we might not be seeing a *true* eradication of rank and status in society through higher education and flow of information. Larger beliefs about economic status, quality of life, and standard of living are often not based on *realistic* assessments. These beliefs, flawed as they are, become instrumental in gaining the confidence the individual needs to get what he wants from life, that is, to be respected, to be in control, and to gain gratification from his social position.

Our theory appears to be vindicated, for there is evidence, from the study of nations alluded to above, which shows that when media influence and academic exposure are increased, young people and other age groups (middle and older) see many things *comparably*. This increase in attitudinal homogeneity between social groups cannot be the result of actual changes, but only in changes in perceptions. When the information culture becomes prominent, one way to describe the overall effect on society is that of thorough-going optimism. Research indicates that the common view in such a society is that people are fair-minded, that they are not rank- or class-orientated, and that the nation has a good future. They are also more satisfied with living at home, but more sensitive to privacy and space issues, and less satisfied with income.

Nonetheless, there are certain differences between age groups. Young adults like to be unconstrained by family imposition, rank, or status, yet they believe that they do not have the *means* to express their power. Thus, they have a greater interest in establishing limits on behaviour through morality. As with young people, older adults have a desire for independence and entitlement, but as they have power, they are more concerned with maintaining a stable social and political environment (domestic and international), where the current system is endorsed (if it were not, then personal aims would be frustrated), and extreme measures are rejected. People in this situation are happier with individual, national and international affairs, feel closer to the political process, but are less committed to others.

These opinions are not determined by all vectors working together with equal strength, but rather some appear stronger than others. Each element covers a certain set of social factors at a particular level of detail; opinions then arise that are commensurate with this purview and level of specificity. For example, the efficacy of the secondary school environment (as measured by students per teacher) has a fairly sizable influence on the things that young people will seek in life, in particular where independence, pride in one's country, social position, and wealth are important. These complex personal goals are formed in the teenage period, when the school environment provides many thought-provoking ideas about situations which directly impinge on social structure. Television, on the other hand, deals with a wide range of general factors, which impact views relating to reciprocal duties of individual and society (such as on fighting for country, morality and future potential). Newspapers are a major source of details about work, politics, labour and business, and so give people ideas on the issues and social interactions in these areas. Books, with their detailed, often historical themes, focus on things not related to the external structures such as work, politics, and economics. They influence how people feel about family relations, ambition, social connections and status usage. College education is quite specific in its influence, and such training gives people the power to say 'rank does not mean everything' because it potentially bestows sophistication, erudition and discipline—aspects which when used properly, can outweigh social status and family connections. Indeed, college education is unique in that it *gives recognisable power* that the other elements considered here cannot.

From the preceding, we draw the conclusion that, in the normal spheres of interaction, *in order for people to feel 'independent' they cannot believe that they are constrained to follow social conventions*, such as delineated by rank, occupation, or profession. People have a vested interest in believing that there are *no barriers to success*, such as rank or wealth. The achievement of social freedom is the raison d'etre for all education, that is, to promote individualistic thought and action, to break the bonds of reliance on other people, and on ideas that putatively hold no value. Thus, increased information flow spreads the 'gospel' that anything is possible in the modern age, and there is usually good potential for success in the future.

Unfortunately, this type of social scenario might interfere with effectively developing companionship. Married life requires both husband and wife to assent to certain conventions and rules as part of the marriage 'contract'. Such assent is made difficult or impossible in a society that is preoccupied with breaking down all 'barriers'. Further, when relatively high levels of communications and schooling exist within a society, then social rank is not usually an openly discussed concept, but independence is still crucially important. In order for one to believe that one is truly 'free', then no person is required to attain a higher social rank, either through achieving milestones in business, or through attaining a certain lifestyle. In this regard, even marriage, if we perceive of it as a lifestyle, is reduced in importance as a status marker.

If marriage is not a significant status marker, then perhaps other forms of status are still important in some respect. We might ask: Does a person's antipathy towards to rank and social position issues also mean that he does not seek *status for himself*? Not necessarily, as long as independence and self-satisfaction are the main goals; if goals can be attained through means other than resorting to the complexities and the commitments that formal social rank brings, then so be it. However, *unofficial* status, as gotten through personal possessions and residential space, and as recognised between two people rather than in some collective way, will always be something that is sought after. 'Status' is unimportant for many, as in the sense of official status obtained through job titles; nevertheless, unofficial status, as obtained through living space and personal possessions, is still critical.

There is a certain irony to this. Although rank and position are not thought to be barriers to success, they still possess high value, in that they are the *reward* for accomplishment, reputation, credentials, diplomas, determination, and work history. Although symbols are meagre items in themselves, without reserving the pedestal and the laurel-wreath as privilege markers for the winners, there is little reason to exceed one's own or others' expectations. Society must have ways of giving individuals the recognition that they have 'beat' others in an endeavour, and even such minor aspects as courteous forms of address or special seats at a table are coveted. Were it not for these factors, the independence ethos would lose force. Of course, there are dangers: Social position can be twisted so that people gain unfair advantage, but it would be foolish to believe that social position ever ceases to be important. Every person has to compare himself to others, in order to understand how he fits in with the larger society.

Hence, the observation that the increase in academics and communication brings some kind of laxity to the social structure does not weaken our contention *that the idea of autonomy is spread with public information*. People are not any less desirous of raising themselves above their peers, and our study shows that people still want to have *power over others*. They want to live life as they wish, and are not likely to believe that work is demeaning and mechanical, meaning that the individual, as far as the ego, or 'I', is concerned, is worthy of respect. On the other side of the coin, when the individual is not 'I', but is someone else, the importance of humanitarianism is lessened. In this situation we find there is less national pride, less desire to fight for one's country, and more social distancing in general. This set of attitudes is not conducive for the formation of a high quality marital relationship. Nonetheless, it might be favourable for the perpetuation of larger social entities, such as government. Democracy is believed to work, because *the individual thinks he has the personal power to influence the rest of society*, to accomplish his aims, and to effect major changes, regardless of how others feel about these changes.

Objectively speaking, these attitudes betray a type of selfishness that leads to great potential *weakness* in the ability to plan for the future. From self-centeredness stems a *cynicism* about one's fellow citizens, such as is shown in a reluctance to defend one's land even though one putatively endorses the national culture. If one believes one 'deserves' a good future, then is it not likely that one would *predict* a good future as well? So logically, one does not feel compelled to defend one's land if one envisions a good future for the nation, as our study found. In addition, to say one is proud of one's nation, because one *believes* there will be a good future, is more than a little disingenuous.

Consequently, *entitlement* is present where opinions form a nexus: People believe rank is irrelevant, they predict a good future for the nation, and the primary goal of the individual is easy enactment of personal plans. *If one really believes one is free*, then one cannot tolerate any restraints, one can simply not be pigeonholed or boxed-in. However, never is there any social situation in which every desire can be easily and legitimately satisfied; thus, logically we can maintain that entitlement, as a product of the desire for independence, creates some level of presumptuousness and arrogance. If you have a long list of 'things I deserve to get and am expecting', you will certainly have to compile a shorter list of 'things I deserved but did not get'. It is how aggressively the average individual pursues fulfilling the latter list that establishes his country's reputation for level of pugnaciousness. Nevertheless, we know from ordinary observation, that bullies often seem indifferent in regards to their prey. The elementary reason for seeming unconcerned about the means to obtain the 'deserved' items on the list might be that such sentiments are signs of *weakness* and/or *failure* and so are considered inappropriate. To say one is dissatisfied implies subordination to a person or institution or system, and this clashes with the modern ethos of independence. When people complain too much, they seem under threat and not free. We mentioned earlier (page 46) that the appearance of being independent is more important that the reality of achievement.

Thus, *if one is to appear 'free', one must accept the status quo, and view society as full of potential to serve one's own ends, with few obstacles or hindrances on one's path.* This produces the sense that one *deserves* to obtain what one *wants*; if this concept were uncertain, then one would not be truly independent within this social milieu. This also relates to issues of living space. When one is raised in a large house, one may succumb to a self-centred attitude, one may feel a sense of *unwarranted entitlement,* of getting what one wants, and ultimately of supremacy over social rules. Where this sense of entitlement ultimately originates is difficult to determine, but probably arises from a collective temperament, economic structure, and history—influences that are facilitated by the media.

It should be realised that even though well-off people have more privacy, this ampleness can potentially foster self-centred attitudes. Certainly, the lack of this cardinal resource can be frustrating and might result in aberrant reactions; still, an abundance of space gives one all the *more* reason to feel entitled, and arouses the feeling that one is not under society's laws. The distinction between oneself and others in such a culturally important aspect, to rise above the rest, can be easily translated to an unwarranted general feeling of superiority. We have said that schooled and media-orientated societies strive to increase space, as informed, aware and knowledgeable people demand privacy. More privacy, however, might often mean more social deviance, as pro-social ideas are often squeezed out by self-centred notions in the information conduits. It might be that having too much space overall is *worse* than having too little.

We can see that behind the issues presented in schooling and media, there is an overarching theme of *man attaining, not just a 'simple' freedom, but a total, complete emancipation.* This affects how the individual looks at relations either with relatives, friends or a spouse. If we can agree that these media, directly or indirectly, consciously or unconsciously, invariably favour the theme of man being independent, free, in liberty and without fetter, man living up to the great Western Enlightenment expectation of being a truly sovereign entity, then we can see how such exposure to communications and academics can produce a sense of entitlement.

It is clear that concepts of personal space and independence are significantly influenced by the flow of information in a society. The ideas that permeate fictional, news and academic works, undoubtedly affect the attitudes of consumers. Although independence is frequently a theme, personal space is rarely so, yet it is often treated symbolically. In fiction, main characters often live alone, or if not alone, then have parties when the parents are out; in other cases, these characters move out to live in small apartments in big cities, where they might be threatened by outside intruders. Despite the fact that they serve the telling of a story, all of these plot devices are treated rather indifferently by the producers. They do not explicitly approve or disapprove of the concepts, but simply weave them into the story, making autonomy a common background. It would therefore be difficult to find unequivocal examples where academics, communications, living space, and marriage are all tied together into one dynamic. Nonetheless, it is apparent that by their ubiquitousness, a clear endorsement of entitlement, of freedom and privacy, is present in all forms of the media.[61]

The findings presented above are consistent with each other, and our major postulates. To summarise, space and privacy can be interpreted differently in reference to marriage depending on the outlook of the individual, his or her education, and standard of living. For a modern society *that is well-educated and affluent, independence is the almost sacred life-principle of the individual, and a lack of space is a challenge to ideas of self-government.* However, this in no way means that the ideal of love is negated, but it is reduced in priority. In this situation:

❖ The tendency is to be independent, and focus on the *present* living situation.

❖ The individual seeks egress if living space is small in general throughout society and in his own home. It is possible the individual might move in with friends as roommates, but it is likely that quarters would be cramped. The individual might prefer moving in with a love interest, since he would be living with someone more amenable and significant. Parents in this society might also be able to afford getting a son or daughter, plus a spouse, an apartment of their own. In either case, the marriage is *hastened*. Thus, when space is lacking, the individual can share space with room-mates but uneasily; it is better for him if he marries, since then he will living with someone who is emotion-ally important to him, and with whom he shares simi-lar interests.

❖ The tendency is to remain at home, if living space is *ample*. The individual has enough space and sees no reason to marry, and so marriage is *delayed*. The indi-vidual can remain with parents at home, or move in with roommates, since any residence will likely have adequate living space for each person. Marriage in either case is not necessary.

Young people in this society are antagonised and threatened by the lack of personal space; to marry early would mean an escape from a too-constricted family household. Their new life might begin in an even smaller place than with the family of origin, but at least it would be with only one other person. Unlike one's parents and siblings, one can freely choose one's spouse, a person one could presumably tolerate much better. If space is available at home, where each child has his or her own sizable room with appropriate amenities, then the impetus to move out to a solitary or shared residence might be eliminated.

In traditional, *less-educated and moderately-educated, and less-affluent societies, marriage is the main aim.* The ability to procure living space can mean early marriage, as couples can obtain their own private residence, producing a more harmonious relationship. Further, when housing is a critical factor, living in a city especially makes leaving home for marriage less likely.[62] In this situation:

- ❖ The tendency is to build up resources in preparation for marriage, and to focus on the *future* living situation
- ❖ If living quarters are *inadequate* in general, and at home, then wait for opportunities and options to arise for adequate living space; parents might not be able to assist in purchase of a residence. All of this acts to *delay* marriage. A limitation of space can mean delaying marriage until space currently occupied by a family member becomes available due to death or departure, or until the couple can save enough money to buy or rent a larger residence.
- ❖ There is a *hastening* of marriage if larger places are available, because one can leave home. Thus, with more space, earlier marriage occurs because of a better housing market (space is cheap) and/or space in the parents' house can be utilised.

The first situation acts as an inducement for early marriage, the second as either a barrier to, or facilitator of, marriage. Where space is available, it is a sign of opulency, and the academic and scholarly 'brain trust', mediated by an extended communications systems, will effectively bring out and reinforce ideas about rights, privileges, social relations, and material values. The less-educated and moderately-educated and moderate-income people do not have

the urge to 'escape' to another living arrangement in order to conform to independence ideals elicited by schooling and communications. There is also no competition within one's extended or virtual
peer group that forces them to develop a sense of entitlement, or
to seek higher status.

In fact, people in the high-education and communications society
will demand that not only a few of their ideals be met, but the
whole set, often in disregard of what the economy and government
can efficiently deliver. When counter-examples to the housing ideal
are present, distressed individuals tend to take the quickest solution, namely relinquishing the companionship of family at an early
age. By having a place of his or her own, the individual has the
freedom to say and do what he or she pleases, without having to
answer to parents.[63]

Studies show that wherever there is interference with the need
for space—which is used for seclusion and temporary isolation, a
place to relax, think, reflect, sleep—there is the potential for psychological and familial disorder. A lack of privacy, in general,
results in lower mental ability, impaired mental functioning, and
greater deviance. This is evidently true of all Western cultures,
regardless of income, government spending, and other forms of
compensation. However, in societies with higher education and
communication, the availability of space, although relieving the
above problems, releases latent attitudes of narcissism, defiance
and hostility. The perspective is something like this: I have a large
house, large rooms, many possessions, I have power over my environment, and other people, both friends and strangers, must find
me attractive, intelligent, and powerful. Of course, there are other
valid reasons that contribute to narcissism and arrogance, but there
is no doubt that the amount of personal living space is one significant factor.

It should finally be noted that it is easy to envision how arrogance can lead to hurt feelings, arguments, rejection of traditional

norms, and self-indulgence. These new difficulties are so strong that they not only negate the positive effects of personal space, but create additional substantial effects on their own. Let us imagine a chart, with space per person on the x-axis and deviance on the y-axis. Traditional and modern societies lie in two 'bands', with the traditional below that of the modern; the two bands begin with about the same space per person, at about the same level of deviance. As nations increase the private space available to the average person, due to industrial and economic development, the two sets eventually part company. Although traditional cultures manage to reduce deviance in relation to more space, modern cultures at the upper end of the range are in a *worse* position. Therefore, the tendency to marry, and so the tendency to 'fall in love', is formed to a substantial extent by the complex interaction between two seemingly romantically barren factors: Housing and social status needs. This is possible, because the most pliable factor of all, mass communication, has become so powerful that it can twist any concept away from its original meaning.

Our examination in this chapter, of how people formulate concepts of privacy and living space has revealed certain unexpected and remarkable facts. An interesting phenomenon has become apparent concerning what is, perhaps, a weakness in human nature: The ability of social factors to exert a major influence on the perceptions and reasoning of the individual, to the extent that his ideals might be altered.

Consequently, in attempting to engineer a *visibly autonomous* life, the individual separates himself from his peers by seeking higher status, through the attainment of greater personal living space, if available. *Marriage itself can be used as an instrument for independence, if it means giving the individual his cherished liberty from a too-small home.* Obviously, seeking egress from the family household is not the only consideration in marrying, but it is a highly significant factor when the concept of freedom has been cultivated. Thus, *the independence ethos, entitlement beliefs, and marriage tendency might logically all be closely related.*

In this chapter, we have seen that concepts of companionship are significantly affected by views of independence, in the form of space and privacy, which in turn are influenced by social factors. By stressing the importance of space and privacy, modern society influences and, in some situations, even encourages people to become selfish, arrogant, and narcissistic, with the result that relationships will suffer, and the possibility of happy marriage becomes less likely. The larger social sphere of culture contains factors which have an impact on the formation of ideas that are important on the individuals's life, whether he is aware of these factors or not. In regard to the activity of conceptual processes, we must now analyse a source of influences that is closer to the individual's life, that of his family of childhood. These influences, because of their proximity, might be more noticeable and manageable, but then, because of their very 'ordinariness', might be ignored.

Chapter 7

The Effects of Household Structure

*P*erceptions of privacy, the need for privacy, and the desire to fulfill that need, besides being influenced by culture, might very well be also affected by factors within the family. Certain family parameters obviously cause changes in living space, such as a large household reduces the individual privacy of its members. Nonetheless, even if space person is the same, living with a large family is not the same as living in a smaller residence on one's own. The effect of being fenced in by four walls is not the same as the presence of four brothers or sisters. Hence, life in a populous household presents some of the more complex forms of interactions, and often the individual has to deal with conflicting forces in his social surroundings that eventually have an effect on his desire for opposite sex relations and marriage. We have already brought up the effect that siblings can have on one another in relation to the propensity to marry (page 11).

However, complexity in the structure of the family of origin, primarily due to a large number of siblings, prompts an individual response that logically could be directed towards, or away from, marriage. A large family might *discourage* marriage, if children perceive that they must, if married, also have a large family, and endure the various problems that are caused by it. This is especially true if the culture of the time encourages large families, but does not provide adequate resources to deal with the burden of the household it advocates. If there is animosity between siblings, people could be induced to stave off marriage as a way of ensuring peace in their own future household. Seeing one's mother having to perform chores for a large family, in addition to perhaps working a part-time job, makes it easy to understand some of the bitterness she can feel at times. Realising that one's father works two jobs, sometimes twelve hours a day, coming home exhausted, annoyed and sometimes injured, is just as disturbing. These observations certainly do not paint a rosy, delightful picture of married life.

The size of one's family not only affects one's perceptions of family life, but also affects the development of one's personality. Constantly encountering people within one's living space, sharing resources and negotiating compromises, can create psychological damage. Verbal and emotional expression can be restricted, in order to hide vulnerability and protect oneself from unjustified attack. The lack of privacy, the absence of warmth and closeness from parents, the incapacity to articulate one's feelings, the barely contained vexation and anger, all might cause especially the younger members of the family to feel frustrated, isolated and insecure. Not surprisingly, research demonstrates that in families where discord and verbal abuse are common, men from such households are more likely to avoid female contact.[64] How can one suddenly become open and congenial to women, when for years such attributes would have meant exploitation?

In spite of these fairly common scenarios, which are seen personally and in the media, we should not expect only one type of result from living in a large family. The dynamics of a large household structure can create, not an aversion to marriage, but a facilitation of it. How can this facilitation of marriage occur? Although constant contact with other members of a household can prevent the formation of constructive self-initiated activities, it does contribute to one's knowledge of the complexities of social relations. Such 'schooling' can be valuable in dealing with the opposite sex in the difficult milieu of puberty and school. In large families, individuals are always dealing with others' problems, helping and interacting. Experience with extensive and varied social interaction is gained, whether one desires to have it or not. Those growing up in smaller families have more time for themselves, but a lack of variety of contacts and situations may cause social skills deficits, and thereby anxiety in dealing with the opposite sex.

On the basis of the foregoing, we can see why large families, in certain cases, would hasten early marriage. People from such families are not likely to be afraid of the opposite sex; larger families usually contain at least one sibling of the opposite sex, thus allowing the individual to have routine personal dealings with them. Consequently, the more children per women, the greater the probability of having both sexes in the household. Men especially seem to need early exposure to females to be confident in courtship. In fact, 'love-shy' (or female avoidant) males are five times more likely to have grown up without sisters, and in homes that were isolated from the kin family network.[65] Males from large families, presumably well informed about the differences between the sexes, would have few qualms or little nervousness about asking girls out for dates, and so the road to marriage might be short.

Further, whilst growing up, an individual from a large family might have little opportunity for private activities, and might become, as compensation, more gregarious or socially-orientated. People from families of only one to three children have more free time for leisure and developing avocations than individuals from larger households, who are often deprived of the opportunity for hobbies, either because their parents did not have the money to supply each child with what he wanted, or due to continual interference from other family members. By the age of 18 or 21, such men do not have pre-existing personal or career interests that consume most of their time and resources. Thus, little substantively stands in the way of becoming a marriage partner, and they might marry early, not wishing, so to speak, to move out of family life.

In contrast, hobbies and other self-based interests give the individual the potential to create something entirely of his own, reducing the need for dependence on another, and so facilitating the bachelor's life and delaying marriage. Such activities can lead to *less* of a desire to marry; indeed, marriage might be seen as standing in the way of such enjoyment.

Thus, if a man has few personal interests, and wants to maintain the positive interaction he had with family members, then coming from a very large household will strongly influence such a person to marry early. There would be little or no hiatus between the domestic life of childhood and that of adulthood, as both would be governed to a large extent by considerations about the welfare of others, not simply oneself. In this sense of foregoing the extended single life, the offspring of the large family structure see the 'traditional' and the 'modern' dynamic as not very different from one another.

Not only are the number of relationships within the household important, but their quality as well. We can deduce that the overall opinion of one's home life has a rather peculiar non-linear relationship to marriage tendency. There is an inverted N-shaped relationship between the presence of *problems at home* (x-axis), and the *desire to marry* (y-axis). Let us take a hypothetical individual who undergoes increasing problems in his family of origin. We posit that when home-life experiences are good (problems are few), this person would want to repeat them, and so he strongly desires to marry some day. As his experiences become more negative, the desire fades; this person has been given an adequate upbringing, and can adjust well to adulthood, but his concept of marriage, although it holds certain attractions, also contains impediments and burdens. However, let us take another hypothetical person, who has even worse experiences; this person will have an *increased* desire for marriage, so as to *compensate* for serious shortcomings that arose in his upbringing. He cannot adjust to adulthood on his

own. Hence, this individual might seek a constructive companionship that he did not receive at home, and this would *increase* the
likelihood of cohabitation and marriage. Finally, as experiences
become very bad, the individual completely puts off marriage,
because he does not see intimate relationships as offering any
positive or compensatory features.

We should make clear that problems with child-rearing might
occur in a family of any size. But if larger families have certain
characteristic aspects about them, then the effects of marriage
patterns on these attributes should be easier to track when fertility
is used; there are no direct indicators of 'family goodness' that
would apply to an entire population. In short, people living in 'high
fertility' circumstances encounter a complex variety of emotions
that are indicative of household dynamics: Dismay about married
life; hopefulness about married life; closeness to one or more siblings; aggravation at the behaviour of siblings; happiness in having
people to talk to; a certain emptiness and anxiety or anger due to
being lost in a 'crowd'. A wider variety of experiences lead the
individual to become more socialised, creating a greater receptivity
to married life, but also inspiring a cynicism about marriage and
people in general. Moreover, culture makes its own contribution
in determining how a person from a large family develops his or
her views on married life.

Three models can describe the interaction between family size
and marriage behaviour. If a large family situation turns out well,
then an individual from such circumstances will be more likely to
marry, based on a positive view of family and good social skills.
However, if the *opposite* occurs and the individual feels neglected
by siblings and parents, he might *also* be more eager to marry, so
as to finally achieve the satisfaction from the much vaunted prom-
ises of hearth and home. This pattern of attraction to, or constellation of ideas about, family life could be balled the *Profamilial
Model*. If family life is perceived as a series of mostly negative

experiences, with interpersonal relation skills also being adversely affected, the individual would assuredly not want to repeat the experience; even if such a person did wish to marry, he or she could not do so easily in any case. The likelihood of such a person marrying early would be small, and the chance would be higher he or she marries late, or not at all. This pattern could be called the *Antifamilial Model*. Finally, if marriage age is *not* determined by the size of the family of origin, but to a large extent it determines the size of the individual's own family (that is, *the direction of causality being the reverse of the other two models*), then this situation could be explained by the *Fertility Model*. Here, when men and women marry early in life, there are more opportunities for pregnancy (the time between first intercourse and menopause is longer), and so there would be more births, *ceteris paribus*.

These three models are equally logical, and appear to be supported by research evidence, despite the fact that studies show only the existence of such models, not necessarily their prevalence. Moreover, the three models are equally likely to occur in a population, given the same background factors. As shall be seen, although a person cannot usually avoid being exposed to problems in their family of childhood, it is the person's *reaction* to those problems that largely determine which model will be followed. The 'seriousness' of a problem is often a matter of personal evaluation, and thus a function of maturity and judgement.

Let us first see what type of environment is engendered in a large family household structure. Studies show that in contemporary Western civilisations, children in large families are raised with less investment by parents, more adherence to rules, less individual attention, and a greater use of corporal punishment. These families produce individuals with lower IQ, lower academic achievement, and lower occupational status; they also produce a disproportionate number of antisocials and alcoholics.[66]

A reasonable conclusion might be made that persons raised in this type of structure would lack maturity, and so would not have the skills to find a marriage partner. The various social deficits possessed by a person who fits the above profile would, in many circumstances, minimise the desirability of that person becoming a companionate partner, and this would delay marriage. Further, such a person might have a very negative view of family life, believing that his own experiences are typical, essentially using his own father and mother as examples of fatherhood and motherhood. If this is true generally, then we would expect to see across European nations evidence of the Antifamilial Model, where higher fertility produces later marriage.

However, social competence is not the only factor, as a man or woman's need for companionship might override his or her negative views of family, and might compensate for personal inadequacies. It is possible then that the larger the family of origin, the greater the likelihood of *early* marriage. We find evidence for this, and further see that having more siblings increases expectations for early childbearing (which would also increase the probability of early marriage, *ceteris paribus*).[67] If a large family produces a dearth of affection in a culture that *otherwise encourages emotional closeness*, then clearly the offspring from large families would rush into marriage to obtain what they lacked at home. They would make a special effort to find someone that they think they could love, and marry them as soon as possible as a way of maintaining that love. Earlier marriage would ensue if the desire for companionship overrides all other considerations, and such a situation would be consistent with the Profamilial Model.[68]

An original analysis of European cultures shows that there is a *positive* correlation between fertility (family size) and marrying young, and a *negative* correlation between family size and marrying later in life.[69] At the very least, this would appear to refute the Antifamilial model, and the Fertility and Profamilial Models are also not to be discounted. We must at least allow for the possibility that the emotional and intellectual effects within a large family encourage marriage. However, as we are also concerned with causal direction, a technique might be used where statistical significance is derived from robust regression.[70] The results of this analysis indicate that it is a large family that often causes early marriage. Specifically, we see that a larger family of origin induces men to marry early, and induces men and women to not marry late. It also demonstrates that early age of marriage for women subsequently affects fertility (presumably their own). To put it another way, *the tendency for males to marry early and to avoid late marriage, and the tendency for females to avoid late marriage, are both driven to a significant extent by the interactions relating to the size of their childhood family.* It would appear that whatever reservations about domestic life people from large families might have are put aside. *Such persons seek companionship and closeness*, quite possibly overcoming psychological problems that had developed in that home life, with an attractive, smooth spontaneity in social relations, a facility learned from living with opposite sex siblings. The Profamilial model now seems supported.

The Fertility Model also appears to operate, but not to an extent that it overrides the importance of the Profamilial Model. Moreover, it is valid only under certain circumstances. Although research shows that women who marry early are more likely to have higher fertility, that is, a large family of their own,[71] this dynamic might not apply across the Western world. Other research that encompasses multinational analyses shows that the dynamic of marriage age as a cause of fertility applies more to men than to women.[72] The reasons for this appears to be connected to the interpretation of 'traditional' concepts of family responsibility.

There are traditional principles of married life that in previous eras were active across the Western world, but these customs have, in general, been abandoned. Nonetheless, some regions and social classes still hold on to them, and they are passed on primarily by family. We might say that a man who comes from a 'traditional' family might be impelled to follow certain behaviours different from others in his society. One such area might be marriage, where if such a man finds the right girl, he will marry early, and then proceed to have more children than the norm. He feels that this is the appropriate thing to do, since it is expected that in married life, the husband and wife continue to have children, until the wife no longer feels able to do so. Whether this perception is actually aligned with the childbearing behaviour of the traditional era (before 1800) is not important, rather what is significant is that there are men living in current times who *believe* that their own behaviour is similar to that practised by their ancestors.

It is possible to integrate high fertility into a contemporary context, but only from a masculine perspective, that is, men marrying young and then proceed to have a relatively high number of births. Women do not seem to follow the same pattern, and if they marry young, additional factors seem to come into play. Hence, although a country might have a relatively high proportion of young men who marry young, their proportion of all married couples, compared to figures several generations ago, is still small. The large proportion of people marrying young in a country does not necessarily make it 'traditional', as other factors must be taken into account. Having numerous children is very rarely nowadays a pivotal factor in the structure of married life, as many of the variables that warranted it (such as using family members on the farm or in the shop, avoiding social isolation, economic support in old age) are no longer relevant, and other factors work against having many children (careers, busy schedules, social disapproval). Thus, the phenomenon of large families is limited in the modern context.

There are also certain allowances that might be made in the case of men. Because it is unusual for men to marry before age 20, people might think that such individuals are dedicated 'family men', and so their larger family is not disparaged. Early marriage for women is not nearly as extraordinary, and so such marriage is no compelling indication of devotion to the family concept. If having large families, or high fertility, is an older traditional pattern, then perhaps the dynamic for relatively large families is drawn from the past, whereas the pattern for early marriage, more from the 20th century.

We have evidence that supports two models, but *each seems valid in different circumstances*. On the whole, the evidence seems to point to the Profamilial Model being most common. There are two scenarios. In one, an unpleasant family life leads people to still have a strong desire to marry, regardless of home circumstances. Because of the frequent but shallow interactions in a large family, the individual might both desire and receive a relatively rapid union. Companionship that was denied in the family might be found in marital life, whereas the communications proficiency gained in that same emotionally lacklustre environment might expedite relations with the opposite sex.

On the other hand, in large families where members get along well, there are warm exchanges that can continue in one's own family, with a wife and children. The greater the number of family members, the higher the chance that there will be positive relationships within the family. This is represented most strongly by nations that differ significantly from the modern average, which makes a difference when it comes to marrying late. Traditional standards emphasise the positive, life-enhancing aspects of family relations, with the implication that the more such relationships one has (e.g., siblings), the happier and more content one will be.

Thus, an extraordinarily 'active' home life no doubt often produces extraordinary individuals, who by their very 'extraordinary' nature are the subject of interest. However, such people are considered attractive not in respect to any great personal moral advantage, but in relation to an uncommon combination of characteristics which eventually end up granting no advantage. The individual uses the asset of skilful social intercourse to gain a certain freedom, but then tends to lose it in a bad marriage, a marriage undertaken in a rush to feed that major liability in his personality, his emotional starvation.

We can see that a large family of origin is still a factor in determining why men will leave home to marry early. The conditions that arise because of the presence of many children in the household are still as valid now as in the past, and economic and other modern circumstances appear not to have eradicated the distress caused by emotional deficiency and a lack of privacy.

In general, it appears that in line with the Profamilial Model, the individual sees family as an excellent source of satisfying social relations, extreme fertility values (large household structure in family of origin) help *establish* the dynamic for marriage (i.e., delaying marriage is not a good idea), but these same values somewhat obfuscate the reasoning for early marriage, because the Fertility Model appears to intervene to an extent.[73]

Our examination of the Fertility Model shows this particular dynamic is applicable in those situations where there are still strong traditional concepts, and those concepts are likely to affect the men in the population, possibly more than the women. Traditional thinking impacts men more than women, and those men who marry early are likely to have more children with their wives. Thus, we can say that early marriage for women does not require the influence of very traditional standards and mores, but early marriage for a man does. Evidently, when men marry early, they are necessarily more traditional in their approach to family life than women, and do not dismiss the idea of having a large family.

We do not find enough evidence to support the general application of the Antifamilial Model. People generally understand that the experiences in their family of childhood *do not have to be the experiences of the family of adulthood*. Nonetheless, it is important to remember that this analysis pertains to people who have great knowledge of other families, and who have freedom in establishing their own lives. They were born in a period when smaller families, strongly growing economies, improving standard of living, increasing life expectancy and better health were emerging as ingredients of a 'normal' society. It is quite possible, however, that our ancestors in the past would have avoided marriage if they themselves had come from large families, as a negative stereotype of the 'tribe-family' had been ingrained in the social consciousness of Western Europeans by the 19th century. The 'duty' to continue family traditions of occupation, family size, inheritance and so forth would have made many large-family individuals quite unwilling to marry, if that is the only way that the 'duty' could have been avoided. Consequently, the social factors that might *discourage* matrimony for a young person coming fresh out of a large household are not prevalent today.

Even if people in our day are raised in a large family, prone to numerous disruptions, they might still have good reasons to marry anyway. Children, although still considered a necessary 'ingredient' to the ideal family, are no longer considered desirable in large numbers, as both parents and their offspring operate under different material and psychological principles. The necessity of intellect rather than brawn for completion of tasks, the availability of pensions and savings for retirement, careers outside the home—all have served to reduce the economic value of a child, and thus the necessity of high fertility. Moreover, society has come to emphasise the individual, and greater attention and time is now expected in educating and nurturing each child. A large number of children would make the attainment of this new social requirement nearly impossible. Further, the concept of family life might not be as tainted by the presence of numerous siblings as it was in the past. Larger houses, more privacy, and a wider range of activities outside the home can now defuse tense family relationships. Even if his own household did not possess the benefits of a well-functioning family, a modern 'mega-family' child could see in his environment examples of families who did. A wider purview is possible because the higher population density and media exposure of our day allows the average individual to come into contact with other households, where no doubt many will be bad, but almost as surely, at least one good, and that is the critical paradigm that our more isolated forbears might have lacked.

These windows on alternate forms of family life make it less likely that men and women who are the products of large families would feel badly about their upbringing; married life, even with many members in the household, does not necessarily have to be a horror, and ways could be found to cope. Therefore, the traditional patterns and constraints of married life have given way to modern lifestyles that allow for privacy, space, material wealth, more direct child-rearing, and quality of child care. For these reasons, the Antifamilial reaction to a large family of origin might have been more common in the generations who lived before the modern period.

We should note that quantitative attributes of privacy and living space have their own independent influences, which we covered extensively in a previous chapter. However, the dynamics of family add further effects that influence a person's views on marriage.

To summarise, our analysis concurs with the position that social conditions in the home have an influence on an individual's psyche, which in turn influences the decision to seek independence by moving out and marrying. A large family, like everything in life, has its advantages and disadvantages, but here the *drawbacks might distinctly outweigh the benefits*; although large families can promote early marriage, what the individual carries with him into that marriage might not be good. It is indisputable that a large family can give warmth, support and security, which create a sense of solidity and predictability in life. On the other hand, greater crowding in the household is often associated with greater *loneli-*

ness, which in turn increases the likelihood of depression and even suicidal ideation.

We cannot overstress the fact that both the *quality* and *quantity* of social interactions are pivotal in the individual's life, and congestion, lack of privacy, and lack of separation, can aggravate the tendency to inflict psychological damage.[74] The individual in these circumstances is not understood, his needs are not met, and so he is isolated emotionally.

If people intelligently used the resources and opportunities life gave to them utilising a viable long-term view, then except in the most crowded households, large families would present a uniquely rewarding experience. Unfortunately, intelligent living, for whatever reason, is not common in man, and a combination of the use and abuse of resources is more typical. The superficial short-sighted reaction to this family situation is most typical: Although a person feels close to one or more brothers or sisters, there are arguments about the sharing of items, use of facilities, intrusiveness, and so on; a larger bedroom or separate rooms might alleviate the situation, but such options are not available. A solution out of this predicament is to marry as soon as possible, even before full maturity and financially security have been reached. The concept of love and the concept of autonomy are thus both put in significant jeopardy.

In the preceding we find what appears to be a violation of a fundamental premiss. The presence of more people in the home does *not* reduce loneliness, but *increases* it when there is not *adequate separation* and when there are poor family interactions. There is little doubt that this is a significant factor when parents, children, and siblings suffer from an inability to show consideration, understand others' needs, enunciate ideas, and compromise. Ironically, the culture of today seems to emphasise companionship (marriage or pseudo-marriage) at all costs, even where there are major personality or psychological complications.

We should point out, that although the quality and quantity of social interactions both have a substantive impact on the development of *negative* psychological traits, our analysis has demonstrated that it is not the number of family members that facilitates psychological *health* and wholeness, but rather the *quality* of interaction between members that matters. Thus, it is easier for a person to fall prey to mental disorders, than for him to gain strong rational, emotional, and creative faculties.

In seeking to more fully understand the dynamics of marriage, we have in this chapter focussed on the individual's relationships with his siblings in terms of how these interactions and exchanges alter, nurture, and satisfy the desire for privacy, as well as for companionship. We have also found that family household structure carries a major potential impact on views, attitudes, and concepts of marriage. A child's personal view of his parents as individuals and role models affects his perceptions of married life. The social context of childhood becomes a factor in how concepts of intimate relationships and companionship are formed. Let us look more closely at the various forms of interaction in families, and how the bonds that are formed take on their unique qualities.

Chapter 8

A Search for Substitutes

*W*ithout question, the way a husband and wife deal with each other and their children, affects the way that their children will appraise married life. Hence, attitudes about marriage undoubtedly form early within the family of origin. If parents quarrel with each other, with relatives, with children, then one might see marriage as a battleground. Every child's life needs to be cultivated to a certain extent, an enterprise which entails providing guidance, supervision, protection, moral instruction, leadership, and material well-being. When this encouragement and nurturance are missing, the child has fewer mental resources, and often views married life as less satisfying. To such a person, 'marriage' is a formidable exertion; he fells that even if a man tries his best to find a good wife, the chances are small that he will succeed. It would make sense for him to put off marriage, and live life his own way for as long as possible in order to forestall the 'dreaded' life. Commentary about the joys of bachelorhood and the difficulties of married life become common in a society where such persons are numerous. Because of the embarrassment of having parents who failed to provide critical emotional and intellectual enrichment, feeble witticisms often taking the place of informative discussion.

In the modern age, there are a number of major event periods that have weakened the family bond. The effects of two World Wars and the Great Depression caused many families to split, because of migration, death or divorce.[75] Fathers were lost on the battlefield, and the ones who came back were often disabled, or had to search for work wherever they could find it. Movement to the cities from the countryside also divided families, and occupational routine changes, technological advancement and labour actions caused fundamental shifts in belief and attitudes. Moreover, the loss of children to war or disease can devastate the remaining family members. The surviving children, seeing this suffering in a unique way, with an understanding not easily available to outsiders, would want to avoid this themselves. Their reasoning is quite simple: If I never have children, then there is nothing to lose, no pain to suffer, no regrets or emotional turmoil.[76] In such a milieu, where parents struggle to keep the family afloat, and deal with the exigencies of the workplace, the children very often receive poor guidance and attention. Individuals from families that witness privation and failure naturally intend to avoid such episodes in their own lives. However, we should note that absence or loss of a parent can occur even in the best of times, and does not have to be due to large-scale events such as war, economic depression, or occupational restructuring. Friction in families, based on selfishness and ignorance, causes just as much, if not more, damage to a child's life, than economic depression or migration.

The macrosocial situation is merely a multiplication of many similar private family situations. Due to the lack of proper mental and emotional development in such households, it would not be unreasonable to believe that social disruption can be an extension of deficiencies in the household. Simply put, disorder in the household produces disorder on the streets. The increase in household disturbances, as fomented by divorce, domestic violence and the dislocations mentioned above, has been tied to a swelling of criminal activity. Clearly the result of antisocial feelings, the disturbing presence of youth-related crime is indicated by the significant increase in under age 18 arrests since 1950. Homicide, the most antisocial act of all, sharply increased in the United States in the first quarter of the 20th century, reaching a peak in the 1930s, declining, then returning to its former peak by the 1970s.[77] Visible in research and anecdotal evidence, the effects of home life are indeed far reaching.

However, there is undoubtedly a *mutual* relationship between society and family, where one affects the other at different times and places. Not only do events in the home influence the behaviour of individuals in the community, but events in the community affect the dynamics of marriages and families. This forms a pitiless cycle, where unsettled conditions in the community cause disruption in the home, which in turn produces even more societal turmoil. As we have discussed earlier (page 16), the stresses of modern life can 'contaminate' the household and induce many to refrain from marriage as a way of preventing such 'contamination'. Nevertheless, as observation of our times can attest, government can only with difficulty prevent the stresses that originate in the household from contaminating society. The onus clearly rests with the individual to keep his home protected, a 'sacred' area of peace and tranquillity, safe from mental intrusions. With responsibility over social problems being constantly passed around, the 'buck' stops at one's own home.

Although the child of a seriously disrupted household might not see his situation duplicated on a large scale, his personal experience is nonetheless painful enough for him to seek amelioration. He might be all that much more eager to marry as a way of finding *compensation for his loss*, consequently obtaining the family life and the love he never had. Perhaps through their own marriage, such people would attempt in adulthood to find the missing pieces of the mental structure that grants emotional independence, a project begun but not completed at home. An additional factor that might propel them into marriage might be an immature outlook, gained precisely from the same poor parental guidance and absence of nurturance that caused the problems originally at home.

We can see that, depending on a person's evaluations and needs, a poor and disrupted family life could lead some people to delay marriage, and other people to hasten it. Such a decision depends to a large extent on an individual's level of maturity, ideas about love, innate disposition to work, level of risk tolerance, ability to plan ahead and impose self-discipline, desire for companionship, and general expectations about what life has to offer.

Hence, one of the most important reasons why one would start courting or dating is to bring serenity to one's mind, by finding a substitute who can complete unfulfilled aspects of guidance, affection and support. Studies show that where a parent is absent, and a household is 'non-intact', dating starts earlier compared to an intact household.[78] The conditions at home often can be strenuous, with a single parent unable to keep harmony without a spouse. Such parents might be unable to make proper decisions without a consort; they might also, albeit unconsciously, push their children to marry as a convenient way of removing them from the roster of household members. Arguments and contentiousness could easily break out as individuals compete for limited resources, against a background of financial uncertainty.

The individual, who is deprived of a sound intellectual disposition, might easily lose interest in a job or hobby. Fulfilling activities are no longer present, and to occupy this void he might turn to doing things that include other people. The need for companionship in a marriage could spontaneously result from the loss of friends, family or others who were close, and afforded emotional and material comfort, advice and protection. This loss typically occurs when the providers of the support, or the one who is supported, undergoes a change in schedule, a different job, or moves away. *Such losses could prompt a search for other means of emotional gratification, which might include a romantic or companionate relationship.*

In relation to individual mental development, often the worst disruption in the family, going beyond separation or divorce, is the actual death of a parent. There are obvious similarities between the life of a person who comes from a family where there was little privacy, due to many children or little space, and a person who loses a parent or other loved one. As we have seen in a previous section, the former experience less attention and affection than people in other family situations, and so do the latter, but with special difficulties. One can possibly repair relationships with parents in a household where there are structural limitations on affection, but one has little recourse about actual physical removal of a parent. Therefore, the most critical of losses is that through *death or departure* of a mother and father. Not surprisingly, the loss of a parent can potentially instigate the strongest effects on the propensity to marry.

From the point of view of the child, a parent can function on a fundamental level as a *friend* and/or *mentor*. The loss of a parent can thus entail losing both someone who provides companionship, as well as someone who educates and edifies. The natural response to losing something is to find a replacement, as good as if not better than the original. After the death or departure of a parent, grandparent, friend, or teacher, an intimate partner or spouse can function legitimately as a substitute. On the other hand, without an appropriate instructor in morals, ethics, and social behaviour, the individual might feel very unprepared to deal with life and close relationships. He might refrain from marriage out of fear of being unable to cope with a spouse and children, and all of the responsibilities that that brings. Our examination here is similar to the one undertaken in the previous section, with people becoming broadly pro- or anti-family; however, we refrain from using these terms since 'family' as a whole is not the influence, but only one or two members who act as individual forces.

In pursuing an investigation of how people react to the loss of a parent, we must differentiate between different kinds of mortality because they impose different kinds of psychological harm. 'Death rate', meaning deaths as a proportion of the whole population, is an indicator of *general* loss, of people of any age group who might therefore represent any role in the family. Because each death in a person's social circle or community might affect a different area of life, it betokens indefinite feelings of disorientation and pessimism. The death of someone who is linked to an age category, on the other hand, signifies the loss of a *specific* role model. Since every age group brings different responsibilities, and since these responsibilities can be grouped into 'role' categories, such as student, bachelor, apprentice, nurturer, confidante, teacher, patriarch and so on, age of death is connected to a particular form of social disruption. Two or more deaths within a particular age category indicate a more intense, or pointed, loss of a role model. A deprivation of overall guidance from one or more persons often follows the demise of an older person, and can engender a retreat, especially when the death is of a father figure. Hence, the impact that death has on the individual is direct and not merely abstract. We can see that in a country where the death rate is higher than average, marriage age and tendency would also be untypical.[79]

Thus, psychological injury in childhood and adolescence influences at what point in their life development people marry. 'Wholeness' in family life comprises moral and ethical support and instruction in cooperative living. *The loss of these components could produce an inadequate or dysfunctional model of marital life and parenthood.* A person who experiences a cessation of parental support and instruction can develop one of two possible attitudes:

(A) A reluctance to form a deep emotional attachment to another person out of fear of committing errors because of an inadequate upbringing, or

(B) A reckless rush into an intimate involvement with another person in order to finish one's personality development, despite being ignorant of the difficulties.

We should first point out that, in studying any changes in death rates, the two effects might be masked by an opportunism effect, that is, people marry because death presents a chance for marriage that did not exist before. For example, if there is an increase in the number of deaths in a community, the marriage rate increases because the newly widowed, with good financial resources, are attractive to people who have been delaying marriage precisely in order to build up their assets. The rush into marriage is not because people want to make up for losses in their own families, but because they are taking advantage of losses in someone *else's* family. If society puts much emphasis on inherited wealth and savings, and not on earned income, then this phenomenon would be expected to occur. In earlier times, when death rates increased, celibacy and marriage age *decreased,* that is, when more people died, more were willing to marry.[80] This fact would appear to support (B) above. However, more people married possibly because a larger pool of available people became present when the death rate rose, thus facilitating matrimony, especially for individuals with high standards concerning financial status and personality. For some, it was not a case of marrying to compensate for deficiencies in the family, but simply a seizing of opportunity that the large pool of 'single' men and women (widowers and widows) offered. This dynamic would not really apply in our day, as the death rates are far lower than in the past, and there are relatively fewer widows or widowers looking to remarry. More importantly, the belief in opportunism in marriage is less prevalent because of the increased emphasis on the individual's money-making ability. Getting rich through marriage is seen as an activity distinctly lacking in altruism. If the belief is present at all, it has taken the form of a 'gold-digging' mentality that has little room for contemplating marriage unless there are substantial returns from the committal.

Another factor might also mask the effect that emotional and intellectual relations within the family of origin have on the choice of spouse and timing of matrimony. In a time of increasing deaths, whatever disorders are killing people, are causing others to fall ill and require assistance, giving individuals more of a reason to seek the support of a spouse. The underlying social phenomenon of this factor would likely be based on a *fear* of sickness and death, which could arise in times of plague or famine, that is, in times of a sharp rise in the death rate. This could work in conjunction with the phenomenon mentioned above, that as more marriages are dissolved due to the death of one member, more people are *eligible* for marriage. Both dynamics can force an increase in the marriage rate when the death rate increases. However, as the year to year fluctuations in death rates are small in modern industrialised nations, it is not likely that more than a very small number of people will take these actions. When the death rate rises, not many men and women will marry early as a result of increased opportunity for wealth (availability of widows or widowers). Likewise, few will marry for the purpose of using companionship as a proactive means of dealing with future or present ailments. A death appears to influence the behaviour of more than one person (a potential spouse looking for material gain, or health provision); mortality also carries an emotional impact where the loss of one person is leveraged, so that the lives of two or more people are touched. A change results in the operational patterns in the household of origin, or a household socially near the individual (for example, that of an uncle or grandparents).

After accounting for these two exceptional situations, we might pose the following question in relation to contemporary standards: Does a relatively high *death rate* in Western cultures entail *late or early* marriage for men and/or women? We should see if analyses of modern data reveal whether high death rates and low life expectancy or whether low death rates and high life expectancy are associated with late marriage and permanent celibacy.

The results from an analysis of Western nations can be summarised as follows (dynamics apply about equally well for both men and women, except for the propensity to never marry, which only applies for women):

Table 3.
EFFECT OF MORTALITY ON MARRIAGE AGE AND THE PROPENSITY TO NEVER MARRY

Mortality	Effect on marriage age (males and females)	Effect on propensity to never marry (females)
+death rate, general	later marriage (weak)	less likely
–death rate, general	earlier marriage (weak)	more likely
+death rate, age specific	earlier marriage	more likely
–death rate, age specific	later marriage	less likely
–life expectancy	earlier marriage	more likely
+life expectancy	later marriage	less likely

Our research shows that people understandably react quite strongly to the loss of a parent or parental figure, more so than when reacting to family size, which was discussed in the previous chapter. A higher general death rate induces men and women to eschew marriage in their 20s, and encourages later marriage.[81] However, using age-specific death rates is more instructive than the general death rate, as they provide stronger correlations.[82] Males and females respond more explicitly to *specific* loss than general loss, but females react less strongly than males in reference to late marriage but as strongly to early marriage.[83] Thus, when it comes to the decision to marry late (over 30), men and women both respond, albeit rather weakly, to general loss of the 'significant others' around them, of whatever age. Not only do many men and women avoid putting off marriage after experiencing a specific loss, but they also show a tendency to rush to form a companionate relationship (marry at age 19 and under), an effect that is equally significant for both males and females.[84]

Another way to measure the loss of significant figures is through the use of life expectancy, specifically for men. The results are similar as those for age-specific death rates. Keeping in mind that the age for fathers that would be critical in raising a family would be between the ages of 35 to 50, a *longer* life leads to *later* marriage, and *lessens* the likelihood of not marrying at all,[85] that is, a negative impact by a family member on one's early life makes one less likely to marry early whilst not rejecting it altogether. Other things being the same, the *shorter* life-span implies a higher death rate, which means that fathers, mothers, or a similar authority figure would die relatively young. This loss stimulates a tendency for some sons and daughters to avoid marrying late, and some daughters to never marry or marry very late (past age 45).

Since age-specific correlations are all positive with early marriage and negative with late marriage, and the general death rates are positive with late marriage, the two types of indicators cannot both be describing the same phenomenon. It is logical to assume that if a single death in any age group causes the individual to delay marriage, then a single age-specific death cannot *also* hasten marriage. Hence, a *single* death's effect on perceptions might not be that significant, but more consistency is obtained when a person experiences *multiple* deaths. More than one death, but in *different* age groups, would cause the individual to perhaps pursue attitude (A) (see page 114); such a person has the ability to deal with issues relating to business, but not to close, intimate relationships. Some disruption has occurred in personal intellectual and emotional growth, but not enough to cause dependence on someone else for completion of 'training'. It appears probable that experiencing more than one death in the *same* age group *reverses* this tendency, and so would impel people to marry. The age-specific death rate represents a multiplier in an age group and general death rate a singularity since it is not likely people lose more than one person in the same age group over a period of a few years. The connections between marriage age and general death rates can be explained by considering the links between age and social roles: The general death rate could indicate the death of a person from any social group, but the age-specific death rate refers to individuals within certain social categories.[86] As the general death rate can be for any age, it is *inclusive* of the specific age groups. By 'any age' we mean any status or role, and so a wider range of possible disruptions can occur, in one case a cousin, another an uncle, another a parent, another a friend, and so on. Modern people, being socially adept, are quite resourceful in gaining knowledge, succour and advice; they can employ people from different age groups, and thus different *social roles*. The loss of someone from one age group can be compensated for by becoming close to someone else, from the same age group. But a loss of two or more people in the *same* age group is more disruptive.

The particular roles of people which are lost within the individual's social circle can be discerned by noting the age groups that peak in correlation (significance), which happen to be the same for both males and females, namely, deaths in the age group 55 to 59 and the age group 70 to 74. These groups would represent, for people in their 20s, the roles of parent and grandparent respectively. Further, robust regression shows that the age of greatest impact on late marriage is 45 to 49, which if a father, would affect a son or daughter as a teenager. We can see that loss can have its greatest power when it occurs at critical points in a person's life. The 55 to 59 age group incorporates parents, and the group 70 to 74 incorporates grandparents. The individual, who was the child and grandchild, respectively, of the deceased, would be around 22 at the time of death, that is, the beginning of a career and independent life. If the parent were in their late 40s, then the affected child would be in puberty. Thus, the loss of a parent or grandparent would most clearly be felt on children who are 15 to 25, and would therefore create the most significant impact on the valuation of companionship.

We should add that although people would most naturally form close associations with parents, it is not uncommon for individuals to have warm relationships with a grandparent, who can be more of a friend than a parental figure, since there is often no necessity for the older person to maintain a higher rank or position of authority. The removal of either figure might make the individual search for emotional counterparts, and this increases the likelihood of early marriage. When figures from *both* generations, such as a parent and grandparent, are lost and in a relatively short period of time, the individual is presumably even more impelled to marry quickly. Hence, a person is most impacted by major loss around the time when significant concepts of the world are in formation and around the time when marriage is being seriously considered. Two or more such tragedies exact a disproportionate reaction, where the total loss is perceived as greater than the sum of the individual losses. Such disruptions in ideas and mental development cause people to seek a companionate relationship for comfort, maintenance and as a framework for a personal evolutionary process that was arrested earlier in life.

Besides attitudes (A) and (B) described above (see page 114), a number of other, less likely reasons could account for the observation that the premature death of a parent leads to a greater likelihood of *earlier* marriage. We know that children rely on parents, but it is quite possible that parents can rely on children. Such reliance might be so great that matrimony is degraded or discouraged, as it would seriously hinder the friendship that has arisen. In fact, a parent might look to a child as a spousal replacement, who can provide the loyalty that was not forthcoming in marriage. Such closeness can encourage a protective (or a 'caged') atmosphere, where in older age, sons and daughters may see themselves as guardians of their mothers (especially if her husband is no longer there), feeling that for the time being, they must sacrifice emotional gratification for the sake of filial duty. When a parent dies in such a close relationship, then the individual would desire a replacement in order to continue to experience close supportive relations, this time with a new, although not necessarily similar, personality. In addition, as an incentive to stay with a parent, the substantial part of an inheritance might be promised to the child who remains as guardian, providing them with a good material foundation for their own life. At the death of both parents, the individual is 'set free', and left with a desire to extend the close guardian relationship, but now with someone else, and utilising newly obtained significant monetary resources. This inheritance dynamic was more common in past times, and is not particularly relevant in our own day; in modern situations, the savings of one generation do not often make for much of an addition to the living standard of the next generation. Beginning in the early 20th century, each generation has enjoyed a large improvement in income over the previous one, so that it has become easier for persons to save or borrow enough money to form an independent household. However, this might change as major structural defects in the economic situation of the early 21st century continue to emerge.

Further, the death of a parent can produce a need not only for emotional support, but also for *physical* support. People generally put great store in patterns of activity, no less so than in the area of health. A son or daughter is the carrier of the genetic material of both parents, and so episodes of physical weakness in either might well be repeated in the offspring. Thus, grave illness in one or both parents in mid-life spurs unfortunate predictions about one's *own* future health. In many such cases, there is dreadful anticipation that the same pattern of illness, with small variations, will befall oneself. In the case of precocious invalidism, marriage becomes an extension of the idea specified in attitude (B) above (see page 114), where 'love' must include critical care during sickness. Hence, the fear of a shorter life span with poor health (either real or imagined) might encourage them to seek companionship as the most important goal in life. The spouse then on many occasions acts as a type of health attendant, in addition to having other functions and playing other roles. Marriage in this case becomes an extremely meaningful life concept, as one's very physical well-being depends on someone else. Yet, other people, with similarly high concepts about marriage, especially when it comes to physical care, might never find a spouse because it is difficult to fulfill the requirements. Even with the fear of illness, they prefer to wait, thinking being saddled with a spouse and children as well as one's own infirmities is worse than only having to take care of oneself, an overwhelming task only in the worst circumstances.

If life expectancy is longer, however, then such emotional concerns might not be important; a devoted partner is not a necessity when one feels one will 'live forever', and so one could be more assertively independent. Marriage is relegated to a secondary, though still meaningful, role, and the individual might marry late simply due to a lack of a good reason to marry earlier. Consequently, the status of one's health is a major concept that can significantly enslave or empower.

We can say that in some cases the *supportive* function of a spouse is eclipsed by what he or she might bring *materially* to the marriage. In essence, the nursemaid is then less important than the business partner. Marriage is not held in such high esteem; one does not have to put off marriage forever because a person cannot be found that aptly fills all personality departments. As in any 'business' enterprise, partners fundamentally operate not on a psychological, emotional or intellectual level, but on a simple material level, and people can therefore be moulded and shaped, they can change to meet the demands of the situation. Thus, the range of choice for potential partners is much greater. On the other hand, some in the same situation might marry late, being too buried in the demands of their life. A spouse might have some attractive qualities, but these are in competition with career, leisure pursuits and revelry.

The larger implications of our discussion can be explored in another work (Sporer 2010B), which examined how conflicts arise in relationships when there are personality, opinion and habit differences, after the attempt to reconcile love and independence is incompetently handled.

In conclusion, to answer the main question posed earlier, it would appear that men and women respond to the loss of emotionally significant figures, of whatever age, by putting off marriage. However, it is likely that *more than one figure must be lost in order for such a factor to have a consistent impact on marriage propensity.* Since the general death rate captures losses from different age groups, the effect of multiple losses is 'spread around', so the person does not feel incapacitated. Nonetheless, when *specific* and *critical* role models are taken into consideration, as in the reaction to multiple deaths within key age groups, such as that of parent or grandparent, the direction changes. At around the time of average or expected marriage age, a loss of a parent or grandparent would make both men and women *want to marry earlier*, not later. We can see that disruption of key personal relationships have a measurable impact on how people appraise married life. Other factors that lead to affiliation with the opposite sex are either ignored or trivialised. Whilst other issues are not to be discounted, *there is little doubt that the loss of a parent or other authority figure has a significant effect on the decision to marry, especially when there is more than one such loss.*[87]

In the preceding sections, we have seen that considerations about space, privacy, family size, living outside the family, and the loss of important family members seem to have profound effects on the desire for companionship, romantic involvement, and marriage. The conclusion to be drawn from our discussions is that men and women are not narrow-minded in the realm of emotion, for they obtain highly significant assistance from each another on a wide variety of matters. But this assistance is not necessarily exclusively obtained from the opposite sex, much less through a love interest. One can obtain help from family members, relatives and friends, regardless of sex. However, the most close relationship, and thus the context in which assistance can best be used, is between a man and woman connected by entrustment within the institution of marriage. What lies at the nexus of all human activity is what one most desires in life, and that is to be loved, and to be loved means to have another pair of hands, guided by intelligence and wisdom, that help reign in the volatile, ever-changing forces of the world.

Most people ultimately rank *emotional satisfaction* over that of intellectual or occupational achievement. We have seen in this and the previous chapter, that if one does not obtain emotional protection and fulfilment at home, because of the confusion that arises out of a large, crowded household, or the death or departure of parents and relatives, *then one will likely seek it in others*, even offering the wedding ring as a means of securing it. Such desire overcomes many obstacles, even the doubts arising from troubling personal family experiences, which by themselves would otherwise effectively hinder marriage.

Chapter 9

The Weight of
Many Influences

$\mathcal{T}$hroughout the preceding sections, we have attempted to identify the factors that determine the living environment a person establishes after he leaves his household of origin, specifically those that are influenced by *material aspects*. By 'material', we mean physical parameters, such as income, expenses, space, but also anything that can bring material advantage, and that would include advice, nurturance and guidance. Of course, we are not denying the importance of affection, personality, beliefs, and other psychological issues, but these issues are strongly impacted by material factors, and it is these factors that have been specifically studied in this book. In this way, we hoped to gain a better understanding of the 'dimensions of companionship', that is, the physical arrangement of the components of a person's life into which love and affection are, hopefully, to be emplaced and found secure. The factors that we have studied were: Expenses related to courtship and marriage; social competence; maturity; concept of independence; amount of privacy at home; type of household structure in early adulthood; loss of a parent and/or other emotionally significant relative.

We would now like to know how these factors work together in combination. It should be borne in mind that variables which otherwise are significant in bivariate combinations, do not necessarily work when put together into one equation. The effect, for example, of two variables acting independently on my behaviour might be well-established. I might have two friends, John and Simon, each of whom exerts a significant influence on my purchase decisions. The more either of my friends insists on buying something, the more likely will it be that I actually buy it. However, if we *combine* the influences of these two friends on my thinking, we find that my decisions then become more unpredictable. If both friends are highly insistent on the appropriateness of a purchase I have in mind, I might become *less* likely to buy it, simply to show that they 'can't push me around'. For the same reason, if both John and Simon are very much against my purchase, I might also resist their opinions. I might then turn to a third friend, whose influence is not recorded, and ask for his advice. Whatever the case, the independent influence of the two friends is not doubted: Each can definitely sway my opinion. But the joint influence of their opinions, if and when it does arise, holds to a different dynamic. Hence, the interaction of social forces, predictable under certain circumstances, is not predictable in others.

In the case of influences on the decision to marry, similar motivations might be found. For example, a small amount of privacy (living space) and a large family size each separately might induce a desire to 'break-out' and then to marry early; however, when the effects of both factors are combined, a desire to *not* marry early might be become manifest. A person might be overtaken by a 'smothering effect' that makes him desperate to reach out into the resource pool of the immediate social environment so as to find solutions beyond the simple or obvious. Thus, marriage and family might be seen as overly taxing, and only some *temporary* companionship might be sought. The resources which such a person calls upon could be numerous and quite varied, and cannot easily be captured within a single analysis.

At the risk of oversimplification, but for the sake of comprehensibility and cogency, we attempt to combine as many as possible of the variables discussed in this book into one 'grand' equation. This will allow us to visualise how these influences might operate and coalesce to affect age of marriage. We find that not all can be combined, but good results can still be derived which can be made understandable at the personal level.

The influences that make people marry young (age 19 and under) and those that make people marry late (30 and over) appear to affect *two different segments* of the population. The former segment might be more immature by nature, less desirous of independence, and the latter might be more developed intellectually and introspective. This is underscored by the fact that there are fewer variables impinging on the decision to marry early, than on the decision to marry late. One would suspect that more mature and intelligent people would take into account more variables in their decision, than people not so endowed.

In the case of early marriage for men, family size and loss (such as through death) of a parent are significant.[88] We might say: If you belong to this segment, if you came from a relatively large family and experienced the loss of a father, you would have had a tendency to marry early. Cordial relations with people are placed higher in priority than social status, and the loss of such a distinguished person in your life makes you seek a substitute, even if this person is not a distinct parental-figure. As your family was larger than usual, you are accustomed to dealing with people, which might facilitate your desire to start your own home as soon as possible, as a way of making up for the lack of affection and support in childhood.

In the case of early marriage for women, family size, recreation expenses, and privacy are significant variables.[89] It could be put like this: If you came from a large family where there was little privacy, but you had the means to enjoy leisure activities and recreation at relatively low cost, you would have experienced a tendency towards early marriage. Perhaps the lower recreation expenses made it easier to meet boys, and see films and other forms of entertainment where intimate relationships and married life were explored in greater detail. Further, like men, you desired to break out and start your own family, to make up for the dearth of affection and attention whilst growing up in a large household. The fact that women in this position have little privacy, being pushed into close living quarters for many years, also contributes to the feeling that in order to become 'adult' they must obtain their own residence and furnishings. However, this must be shared with someone else for the purpose of making it meaningful and stable. Interestingly, for women the loss of a father does not contribute one way or the other to the decision to marry early.

Late marriage for both men and women is influenced by family size, privacy, the loss of a parent, and recreation expenses.[90] Thus, the segment, more refined, knowledgeable, and intelligent, would probably marry late. The following scenario might be present: You grew up in a small family, with a great deal of private space for yourself, and, since social status is important, you feel privileged in this regard since you have enjoyed good familial interaction. However, you were hindered to an extent in meeting the opposite sex because of the high cost of socialising. You had the opportunity to develop your own rewarding activities, with the result that you feel others respect you for your character and accomplishments. Nonetheless, the loss of your father definitely made you feel more isolated, because this type of occurrence has not happened to any of your peers; you felt different, and thus less involved in relationships with them. Also, this loss made you feel that you had not obtained as much instruction about life, making you reluctant to start intimate relationships, out of fear of making serious mistakes that would make you look foolish. This attitude fits in with the rest of your personality, which demands discrimination, reflection, and adequate preparation.

We note that the variable we use as a proxy for loss of a father can either have a negative or a positive influence on late marriage, depending on whether this variable is used by itself or in conjunc-tion with other variables. It would appear that two different seg-ments of the population interpret this differently. For those who are not status-orientated, and thus who do not take privacy, family size, and expenses simultaneously into account in their lives (that is, they are not using the multiple variables as described above), but who are still people-orientated, the loss of a father clearly means desiring that a substitute be found, and so marriage is has-tened. The loss of one relationship demands the setting up of a similar or replacement relationship. But for those who are more status-orientated, more sensitive to external judgements, the loss of a father means to delay, not hasten, marriage. In this case, the loss of the father, when taken *in conjunction* with other factors of import to the individual, creates the sense of delayed maturity, of an incomplete up-bringing. Consistent with this outlook is the belief that small families and privacy are part of a superior lifestyle.

Before we finish this section, it behoves us to make two points about the applicability of the above analyses. We have already suggested that it is likely that the type of individual we have been discussing is not entirely ordinary, especially the late-marrying person who soberly considers several or more variables in evaluat-ing his or her life. Such individuals are more likely to be deep thinkers with a penchant for unconventional solutions to problems. For imaginative, introverted people, a rich inner world can be constructed if enough personal space and privacy are available. Through books, television and other media, situations pictured in the mind provide contact with imagined friends from other times and places, who can become substitutes for the inadequate social relations of the external world. The loss of a parent, and the re-duced social interaction in the household, might actually necessi-tate such a construction. Far from being pathological or strange, such mental fabrications can vastly improve a person's life, and just as importantly, prevent imprudent involvement with the opposite sex. Thoughtful people, who take into account a multiplicity of variables, are also more likely to build such an inner world, more so after the loss of a parent. This world creates a refuge, thus delaying or largely obviating marriage.

Moreover, although many in a modern population have experienced one or more of the negative living situations described above (large families with four or more children, the loss (eg. death) of a parent, very small living space), there are many others who have not. Yet, there is little doubt that the *elementary factors* of attention, advice, privacy and support have, when held back, an effect on *all* people. These underlying forces can only be observed when they manifest themselves in certain ways, putting limitations on the analysis of international data. The limitations are not necessarily applicable in real life; we should, whenever possible, focus on basic dynamics, not on the manifestations.

However, we should not think that the factors that constrain our analysis also limit the scope and expression of that factor in everyday life. For example, the problems produced by the death of a parent are similar to those caused by parental abandonment, divorce, separation, or inadequate attention due to excessive overtime and travelling. The tendency to seek alternative means of support outside the home might be, in these cases, significantly increased, although not as much as if that father had died. All situations relate to the *same* basic underlying factors which then affect the child: Loss of support and advice. Consequently, he or she 'evacuates' to an alternative relationship earlier in life, abandoning the family relationship, when the home situation is not supportive enough, whatever the actual reason.

The phenomena we have been studying can potentially affect large numbers of people, when the factors are correctly defined and understood. For instance, the term 'loss', whether it pertains to the removal of privacy, attention, affection or support, can have a wide range of meaning and differential levels of impact. Accordingly, the factors that we have studied here exist in some quantity in the lives of all people. Quite simply, certain social forces apply to everyone, and cannot be ignored.

As the contours of the present time resolve into shape, often we find distinguishing features that separate it from the past. We ask: What new world have we discovered on our adventure, to what land has the ship of modernism sailed? As long as the new country provides plentiful harvests, the people have seen fit to leave the problems of love and marriage to the individual. Our attitude, of course, is not so indifferent. We note that the children born in this new land treat socialising, courtship, and recreation differently; they are insistent on early departure from the home of childhood; they are more arrogant and materialistic about life expectations; they have more unattainable ideals; and they have less virtue. What still remains from the country of forbears are a number of factors: The immutable ideal of love, with its concomitant emotional fulfilment; the importance of parental companionship in childhood; the critical need for both similarities and differences between spouses; and the centrality of sensible economics in life of the marriage household.

However, the long-term viability of modern marriages is much in doubt, affected as they are, at least in part, by factors totally *unrelated* to the background, interests and concerns of the couple. Since the aspect of the relationship that delivers affection and fulfilment is now potentially disturbed by thoughtlessness and opportunism, we are compelled to examine the fundamentals of relationships, and how they have been impacted by the source of this selfishness, namely the modern independence 'ethos'.

Family relations, ambition, personal freedom, status, the desire for intimacy—all are highly important concepts in everyone's life. Yet integrating these components is difficult. We have attempted to think in an original manner, in order to understand how these factors interact to form major life choices. We posited that marriage has traditionally been the main relationship in which these features can be harmonized, and Western society has offered viable pathways where a succession of accomplishments can bring about happiness. Hence, it is possible to integrate personal needs, while at the same time handling difficult material demands. Nonetheless, the individual has to discover the factors that could hinder his progress. We have discussed why people tend to overvalue their expected success in career and social pathways, and undervalue the role of chance and natural aptitude. A person might leave his or her home to begin a new life situation, but the living arrangements that ensue are often less than satisfactory. The research that we have cited indicates that a desire to create a intimate relationship can be the result of a lack of privacy, a large family, or the loss of a parent; a relationship is therefore sought that will provide the emotional and mental support that was lacking at home. This might override the rational considerations that are behind the choice of education and career. However, to the individual, it is just as rational that he find an emotional gratification that he knows cannot be found in the institutions in which he studies and works. Many people in the world might see the strong desire for intimacy as being 'irrational', but such desire is legitimate, and thus the seeking of it is indeed rational.

We can state that the desire for intimacy carries more weight than material factors; even today, with an understanding of moral values and intrinsic psychological factors, one can attain a companionate relationship that brings respect and consideration, despite limitations in the family life in childhood. What still remains to be studied are the underlying personality factors that contribute to creating a bond between a man and a woman, some of which, whilst remaining unchanged in their effectiveness, have been unwisely re-prioritised or ignored altogether. It will be apparent that over the last two centuries, the parameters of male-female relationship, usually discreet in nature, and only infrequently of interest to national officials, have undergone a transformation. The enormity of the changes makes it difficult for the designated leaders of modern materialistic society to claim that unhealthy marriages are beyond serious public concern.

The solution to these issues is to promote in individuals, firstly, a greater consciousness and awareness of their own personal ideal of companionship; secondly, an understanding of their social environment; thirdly, the appropriate utilisation of resources that would make the ideal come to life. All of these components interact, and one is not more important than the other. Modern people must attempt to be idealistic and realistic at the same time; one must not be 'tempered' for the sake of the other. In this way, and only this way, can men and women find true fulfilment in intimate relationships.

Notes

1 Tokareva 1987; Bernard 1982.
2 Veenhoven 1983; suicide rates for the Netherlands.
3 Blossfeld & Jaenichen 1990.
4 Elder & Rockwell 1976.
5 It would appear, though, that Catholics are hardly conservative in all matters. In a Gallup poll published on 16 May, 1985, when asked if premarital sex was wrong, 46% of Protestants thought is was, compared to only 33% of the Catholics. One could argue that Catholics are willing to tolerate premarital sex precisely because they consider marriage such an important aspect of life. Cohabitation for the sake of 'trying out' various partners for a good relationship 'fit' might be consistent with the ideal of lifelong marital gratification, more so than marrying without experiencing prior intimacy. However, this *does not work* in practise, as those who cohabitate and then marry have a *higher*, not lower, chance of divorcing. It would appear that one can quite adequately obtain all the information necessary about a person without having to reside with them, and those who do cohabitate do so largely for reasons unrelated to affection, love or long-term stability.
6 Stycos 1983.
7 One should be careful not to conclude that the unmarried are generally more irreligious, as we are saying here only that there are more unmarried persons among those with weak *religious* beliefs. It is likely that people first become disenchanted with religion, then become disenchanted with marriage; although the direction of cause and effect could work the other way, it does not seem to be the case.

8 Hertel 1988.
9 Kilmann et al. 1993.
10 Prokopec 1977.
11 Bolger et al. 1989. The frequency of domestic conflict is naturally dependent on individual reports, which are probably not entirely accurate.
12 Malony 1988.
13 Bachrach 1980.
14 Ramu & Tavuchis 1986.
15 Chadwick & Heaton 1992, Table C3-5, p 97.
16 Herlihy & Klapisch-Zuber 1987, p 323.
17 Sporer 1999.
18 Buck & Scott 1993.
19 Wrigley 1987, p 236-237, Figure 9.6.
20 Sporer 1999.
21 U.S. Bureau of the Census 1992, p xvi.
22 It would appear that compared to other industries, the service industry in the United States is more unequal in terms of income distribution than in the rest of the Western world (see Sporer 1999). Greater employment in service industries *reduces*, not increases, income inequality throughout the Western world, by decreasing the income held by the top 10% of households. Moreover, working in a service industry makes it *less* likely that women will remain permanently single. Working in such industries appears to attract women to marriage, which is consistent with the idea that equal distribution gives *more* hope for the future, and thus acts to facilitate marriage.
23 Temple & Polk 1986.
24 Jencks et al. 1983.
25 Teti et al. 1987.
26 Blossfeld & Jaenichen 1990.
27 Buck & Scott 1993.

28 Goldscheider & LeBourdais 1986.

29 This might very well contribute to the high dissolution rate for marriages where one partner is below 21. There is justifiable uncertainty as to whether the decision was made by 'adults' or mere 'children', although the married life and the consequences of divorce most assuredly require a mature disposition.

30 Goldscheider & LeBourdais 1986.

31 Goldscheider & Goldscheider 1989.

32 Buck & Scott 1993.

33 See Chadwick & Heaton 1992 (Table D3-1., p 119) for evidence that the percent of never-married women with one or more children has grown greatly since 1960, regardless of education. Furthermore, even in married households, parental absence is not at all unlikely; less than 6 in 10 marriages can be expected to last 20 years, that is, for the whole childhood of even the oldest child (ibid, Chart C1-3., p 86). Similar statistics can be adduced for many other Western nations.

34 Buck & Scott 1993. National figures for unemployment are evidently more daunting to the average citizen than local figures. At least if local unemployment were high, the possibility remains of the person finding a job outside the area, but if national joblessness is a problem, then the chance of *finding work anywhere is low*.

35 Data taken from Leppel 1987. The table, labels (Conservative and Liberal), and the discussion that follows, are our own.

36 Leppel 1987.

37 Grigsby & McGowan 1986.

38 Sporer 1999.

39 ibid. This applies when the proportion is of the whole youth population, not just the unmarried.

40 ibid.

41 ibid.

42 Koller & Gosden 1984.

43 Palisi 1984.

44 U.S. Bureau of the Census, 1989, Table 690.

45 ibid., Table 1233.

46 ibid., Table 1235.

47 Carter & Glick 1970, p 138.

48 It is important to note that high housing prices might *not* alter the desire for a separate residence. In Spain of the late 1970s, people adjusted their timing of marriage rather than the context of marriage itself. Marriage in such situations is deferred until adequate money is saved (Stycos 1983). In contrast to Spain, people living in Eastern Europe might put a premium on marrying early and/or having children, and thus will do what they can with regards to housing, even if it means living with family. Clearly, the decision to live alone is a function of individual temperament, and is not that amenable to cultural pressure, unless cultural principles are the product of a collective Will that is allowed to legitimately express itself. Hence, the desire for companionship, the desire for children, the desire for privacy, housing prices, and savings rates, are all relatively independent factors that must be connected in the correct causal sequence.

49 Ideally, there should be little or no correlation between housing and marriage rates. This, however, is rarely, if ever, attained. Nonetheless, society should stand firm in keeping housing reasonable, instead of allowing prices to rise, as they did in the 1970s. Since residences are allowed to be bought and sold freely on the market in most places in the Western world, the blame for the inflation in house prices can be laid on both buyers and sellers. If young

couples are strongly motivated to obtain a place of their own, they would be willing to sacrifice a greater share of their income, rather than go without that first independent residence. Yet, once having gotten their own home, these same couples will then complain that they do not have enough money to make ends meet. The psychological dynamics behind consumer pricing strategies is worthy of study, because it appears *that people do not act rationally in balancing their interests.*

50 Sporer 1999.

51 ibid.

52 Those who watch *C-SPAN*, *Nightline*, and Sunday morning politically-orientated interview programmes such as *Meet the Press*, are normally from the higher income and educational echelons.

53 U.S. Bureau of the Census, 1989, Table 708.

54 ibid., Table 378.

55 ibid., Table 396

56 ibid., Table 708

57 ibid., Table 396

58 ibid., Table 396

59 Sporer 1999.

60 A series of questions was given in 1978 in seven Western European nations, to young people ages 18 to 24, with an average age of about 21 (Gallup 1978, pp 373-402). Although the details of our analysis are not reproduced here, we can conclude that *greater communications and education* (* denotes statistical significance): *Increases* the desire to live one's life as one likes (the independence ethos); *increases* willingness to attribute dissatisfaction with home life to inadequate *living space*; *increases* likelihood of saying that morals are lax; *decreases* overall dissatisfaction with household life; *decreases* discontent with

present household income; *reduces* willingness to say social rank, position or *wealth are important to attain personal success or are major goals; *decreases* willingness to
say one can only carry out mechanically one's job at work;
increases willingness to see a good future development
for the nation.

For the attitudes of a population with an average age
higher than that above, we obtained survey data from 12
nations (Hastings & Hastings, 1987, pp 562-587). We find
that *increased communications and education* are associated with: A *lesser* belief that there will be war in the future; *more* happiness; a *greater* desire to defend the current political system against change; *less* desire for a *radi-
cal change to the system, or to associate with extreme left-
wing politics; *more* satisfaction with democracy; *closer*
affiliation with political parties; *less* willingness to fight in
a war; *less* certainty about whether one is proud of one's
nation or not.

61 Unlike the mainstream media's frequent coverage of the
effect of films and television on society, academia's interest is lacking in uniformity. The theme of autonomy in
particular seems overlooked, although there is good evidence to show that it is one of the top philosophical concerns behind plots and characters. Research demonstrates
that Western culture puts great emphasis on freedom,
family, rights of man, and democracy. The French people,
for example, believe that freedom is the most meaningful
thing in life, with work and love forming a second tier of
interest, and then money, happy family and friendship
(Hastings & Hastings 1987, p 511). Consequently, the autonomy of children, portrayals of the ideal woman, and
disintegration of the family were common subjects on
French public television programmes. Further, two main

categories emerge in relation to these subjects: Social problems relating to exclusion, and problems involving disintegration of relationships (Chalvon-Demersay & Libbrecht 1995).

Hence, the themes of independence, youth, family, and rebellion are often interrelated. Genre films that focus on robust, determined actions, can address these basic subjects better than other, more general, types of film. For example, Americans enjoy Westerns because they unabashedly portray an ideal life consisting of freedom and closeness to nature, which is unique and a well-established part of the nation's history (Shively 1991). This scenario is hardly a utopia, however, as various forces constantly intrude and threaten to destroy family and individual. Horror films take the fears in Westerns and bring them out into the open. Common themes such as alienation, confrontation, separation from family, as well as autonomy, are often successfully presented (Farquhar 1992). How much support is given to the concept of autonomy is difficult to determine, but it would appear that films find it weakening in influence, since one of the dilemmas consistently returning to haunt male characters is to have their masculinity under attack (Lipsitz 1990). Certainly, breaking free of restraints (such as most developments in a modern person's life) is a bold enough step requiring a more characteristically male response. One could say that ruggedness, alienation and disruption of relationships are invariably related to the struggle for autonomy, and so it would make sense to link these topics in fictional works.

Many observers of the film industry would argue that the primary purpose of the movie, indeed of any fiction, is to present an escape from ordinary life, a temporary diversion, mere entertainment. The audience member wants to get lost in someone else's problems for a change, he wants to see the 'little guy' win, but he has no interest in seeing anything relevant to his own life on the screen. However, considering the theme we are discussing, it seems unlikely that people would be quite content to sample something so elemental as liberty or autonomy only in movies and not want it in their own lives. Of course, in the case of genre movies, many plots involve situations that are not part of the average person's life, and people do not expect to be confronting Apache Indians or killers wearing hockey masks anytime in the near future, but even there they *do* identify with the need to lash out at whatever is holding them back in life. People can and do abstract the major themes from a particular context, whether in a film or in life, thus building a bridge between reality and fiction. In fact, if films are designed to connect with a person's experiences rather than offers an escape from them, we would precisely expect them to focus on *freedom* and not fantasy as a major concept. There is compelling evidence that both concepts are popular, but more socially relevant and critically acclaimed films usually possess the former.

As powerful a medium as theatrical films are, it is no longer the most socially important form of art, competing with television (Liehm 1975). The range of sources that propagate the above themes has been enlarged. The superior availability of television compared to major motion pictures makes the themes presented therein to be even more influential. Television, it has been found, is powerful enough in assisting young people in forming an identity and developing ideas about autonomy (Corset 1995). Ideas about independence have been successfully inculcated, at least in part, through the frequent depiction of high-status, supposedly highly autonomous occupations; the audience encounters characters holding such occupations more often than they would in real life. Lower status occupations, when portrayed, are also unrealistic, in that they contain more latitude than is true in real life (Berk 1977).

Obviously, a substantial work could be devoted to the theme of independence in films, television, magazines, novels, newspapers, and so on. What is clear is that the theme is so prevalent that one could be justified in saying that it is omnipresent. Whether it is cowboys on the range, defending themselves against encroachments by the big ranchers, or hustlers trying to stay alive in a grimy New York environment, or men encountering nearly invincible creatures in the depths of space, film and television consistently show the individual in challenging situations; the group has failed, and now it is man alone who must succeed. As Hitchcock observed, most movies are basically about ordinary people in extraordinary situations. Modern stories all in one way or another feature a loss of rights, liberties or opportunities, which could be due to illness, an escaped convict, a major corporation, officials working as part of a government conspiracy, or simply fate dealing a poor hand. Whatever the details, the story must present the individual struggling to retain his dignity, social position, and sometimes his very life. Any significant loss of freedom is a loss of identity, not only for one person but for all people; 'giving in' to the 'dark' forces in any way endangers us all. The whole edifice of the media attempts to link individual struggles with the universal struggle for autonomy, by showing that the ordinary person's life problems are really not different from the ones that are seen on the screen. Television and theatrical films have recently tried to take the impact a step further, by often saying their production has been 'based on real events', or a 'fact-based story' or is 'inspired by a true story', making even the most incredible situations that much closer to the life of the viewer. Whether the source is film, television, book, or magazine, the contemporary fictional story strikes a responsive chord in the viewer or reader using a variety of devices, and the anxiety the individual feels is almost always more to do with a subconscious fear about the loss of independence, rather than worry about characters, or identifying with a storyline.

62 Buck & Scott 1993.

63 It would appear that when people are heavily exposed to the media, as well as being more desirous of independence, they become more aware of the social environment. For example, women who watch television more heavily tend to be more socially orientated; they would also like to be more aggressive and to show more leadership (Gutman 1973). The medium provides nourishment to extroverted and gregarious people who seek out ideas about trends, issues, and fashion. Clearly, leaving home to marry or live with someone is a social statement, decisive, and perhaps more than a little bold, thus neatly tying together the various desires kindled by media sources, such as television. A small living space would be sufficient impetus for this process.

64 Gilmartin 1985.

65 ibid.

66 Wagner et al. 1985.

67 Elder & Rockwell 1976; Trent 1994.

68 Of course, we should be careful not minimise the effects of other factors in these fundamental decisions.

69 Sporer 1999.

70 ibid.

71 Wagner et al. 1985.

72 See Sporer 1999. In order to derive significant results showing early marriage as a cause for higher fertility for females, the highest fertility rate country in the set, Ireland, must be removed; to obtain significant results for males (both early and late marriage), and females (late marriage), all countries must be left intact. The common factor for both men and women is *early* marriage, which prompts us first to ask: Why would the dynamic of early marriage for women be weakened when Ireland, with its relatively high fertility rate at the time of analysis, is left in the set? The people of Ireland do not seem to connect marriage age and fertility in the same way as do people in other countries. Whilst it is somewhat risky basing our observations on only one country, because the country in question is so distinctly different from others, we can make some conclusions. Ireland has been known to be a 'traditional' country by virtue of its social standards, that is, at the time the data were collected, it had no legal divorce, no legal induced abortion, low overall crime rates, and, last but not least, a considerably higher than average fertility. Paradoxically, Ireland was ahead of other countries in its 'modern' fertility rates, in that although it had achieved relatively low birthrates by the turn of the 20th century, these rates decreased little compared to the declines occurring in the rest of Western Europe. Ironically, by the 1970s, Ireland had the *highest* fertility rate of any Western European nation. Occasionally, one finds oneself somewhat embarrassingly the subject of attention, not because one has moved into the open, but because the other members of one's group have taken two steps back. The grave situation of the 19th century, which forced the

birthrate down, gave way to a more stable times which stopped the birthrate from falling. If the twin evils of over-population and famine had never occurred, then it is quite possible that Ireland would have been similar to other nations in its birthrates in the period between the mid-19th century and early 20th century.

What distinguishes Ireland from other traditionalist countries in the set (such as Spain, Greece, and Italy) is its high fertility and its only *average* figure for percent of brides who are 19 and under; we would expect this latter percentage to be high. The dynamics of *strongly traditional nations* might be well outside the ambit (sphere of influence) of contemporary standards, and fertility above a certain level is determined by other cultural factors.

On the other hand, if we were to believe that fertility induces early marriage age for women (something that the analysis above does not support), leaving Ireland in the set *reverses* the dynamic. Having a small to moderate family of origin makes women marry later, but having a distinctly larger than average family of origin would induce women to actually marry young. Thus, when families are not too large, then the Profamilial Model applies, but if they go beyond a certain size, the Antifamilial Model is applicable. Although this is a reasonable assertion, after judging the evidence in the contemporary context, it appears that this dynamic if it exists is not especially strong.

In other words, Ireland's set of social standards is different from that of other nations, even ones influenced by traditional mores, and these standards prevent a significant association between marriage age and fertility in that country.

73 One of the problems we encounter is in the definition of 'large family.' Obviously, there is no clear dividing line

between 'moderate size' and 'large size.' Our statistical analyses demonstrate a smooth linear correlation, meaning that we are not dealing with conscious 'grades' of family size, but rather that the dynamics of the family itself increase proportionately with its size. Further, there is no convenient way to determine 'early' or 'late marriage.' These can only be considered approximate gauges of marriage propensity.

74 Wenz 1984.

75 The problem of divorce is hardly recent. On top of an already disturbing trend, the number of divorces rose sharply during and just after the Second World War, then dropped back down to the pre-war trend (Chadwick & Heaton 1992, C1-1., p 85). In other words, the divorce rate in the 1950s and 1960s would probably have been at the levels recorded even if the war in Europe had never occurred; the dislocation of war (and carelessly arranged, rushed marriages) simply accelerated the pace of divorce for a time, but the trend had started all the way back in the 1880s. The temporal depth, and hence the complexity, of the divorce dynamic is quite extraordinary, and a call is made for the careful scrutiny of a most remarkable phenomenon. Moreover, it would appear that many men, women and children were already being heavily affected by marital separation and dissolution in the middle part of the 20th century.

76 Another factor that determines how people look at marriage is the structure of the household itself. If a mother is at a distinctly lower level than her husband, female children might opt to delay or forego marriage. From their personal experiences, they have formed a negative view of marriage and they would prefer their freedom over having a husband dominate them. This scenario is made

more likely if a mother wanted to work, but was forbidden to do so, or if she wished to have other activities outside the home, but was thwarted. Whether such actions are typical is less important than what the individual perceives (rightly or wrongly) about her future.

77 U.S. Bureau of the Census, 1975, Table H Column 972; Table H Column 1006.

78 Coleman et al. 1985.

79 In this analysis, death rates and marriage rates will centre around the mid-1980s. The effects of a death would be nearly instantaneously manifest on those remaining. There might come years between that death and the decision to marry, so a person marrying in 1987 might be reacting to a death that occurred in 1977. We should point out that this lag should not be a major problem, since a country's rate in one particular year is probably indicative of a fairly stable tendency, which is precisely what we seek to understand. Although indicators often change in absolute terms, they do not often change in rank. A nation, when compared to other nations, might have had a relatively high death rate earlier in 20th century, and it would probably have a relatively high death rate again at the present time. However, that nation's rate has decreased considerably in absolute numerical terms. Hence, a nation's death rate for a particular year shows it mortality 'tendency' (or propensity) as much as its marriage rate show a marital 'tendency' (or inclination). Rates might decrease in numeric terms, but the tendency for an action remains the same as long as ranking remains the same. Correlations between rates are only to be taken as approximate indicators, not precise guides.

Moreover, we should keep in mind that age of marriage in modern European cultures does not necessarily mean age of first marriage. Our ability to determine whether delaying marriage helps people form better marriages, with lower probability of divorce, is confounded by the fact that divorced people who remarry tend to be over the age of 30. As most marriages break up from age 30 and up, and since most of these people remarry, a substantial proportion of these late marriages might be second marriages. The correlation between marriage at the age of 30 or older and divorce is positive and significant (Percent marrying 30 or older x Percent divorcing as percent of marriage age population, $R^2 = .3598$, $p = .0031$, $F(1,18) = 11.68$). This dynamic hampers, to an extent, the differentiation between the reasons for marrying. For example, is one marrying late because marrying for a second time usually comes later in life, or is one marrying late because one is delaying a first marriage? In most countries, however, divorce, as of the mid-1980s, was not so high as to render our results invalid. It would also appear that even when people remarry, they might do so as a reaction to loss of a parent or other figure, since many after divorce will rely upon, or even live with, such people. In essence, they go back several steps in life, to the time before their marriage.

80 See Kuklo 1991, for evidence in the decrease in celibacy rates in Warsaw after the rise in mortality caused by the war, floods, famine and plague of the mid-1790s

81 Sporer 1999.

82 ibid.

83 ibid. Females show less correlation with age-specific deaths than males, at least for late marriage, as shown in part (b).

84 ibid.

85 ibid.

86 General death rate does not appear to be a good indicator
   of how people react to loss. Let us look at an example.
   There are two nations, *A* and *B*, where we assume that the
   death of a middle-aged parent leaves one child troubled.
   If Country *A* has a *higher* death rate for middle aged (45-
   49) parents than Country *B*, Country *A* will have relatively
   more people affected by this loss. However, if we looked
   at the two nations' overall death rates, they might actually
   be similar because of the difference in the *size* of this age
   group. Although Country *A* might have a higher age-specific death rate, the effect on the overall death is negated
   by the smaller percentage size of this age group in the
   population, compared to Country *B*. Thus, some effects
   will be obscured if we do not control for the size of age
   groups.

87 One could look at the connection between mortality and
   marriage from the perspective of a life-prolonging influence engendered by living in close proximity with a sympathetic and supportive person. In this case, the opposite
   direction of causality might be appropriate, that later marriage might result in a higher death rate. There is evidence
   for this dynamic, and no doubt marriage has helped many
   people lead a more comfortable and longer life. Nevertheless, the existence of one dynamic does not necessarily
   negate the existence of a dynamic whose causality lies in
   the opposite direction. Our analyses show that age-specific
   death rates are *positively* correlated with early marriage.
   If marriage has a clear beneficial impact on health, then
   there would be an even greater extension of life than is
   the case with marriage later in life; instead, there is a
   shortening of life for people who marry young. Both the
   death rate and percent who are over 30 at marriage variables are taken from the mid-1980s, very close to each

other in time. It seems doubtful that the effects of marriage would manifest themselves in a lower death rate almost immediately; one would rather expect a lag of perhaps twenty years or more. Hence, the direction of effect should be the other way around, where deaths influence marriage behaviour. More likely, recent deaths of family members would have more of an impact on marriage practices, since the latter are far more flexible and amenable to change than matters of health, a notoriously intractable and slow-moving dynamic.

Consequently, it appears quite unlikely that one could derive some kind of mid-life prophylaxis from a marriage begun only a decade earlier, as there is little evidence that health effects would manifest themselves so soon after marriage. Marriage would then be a lifesaver, indeed!

88 Sporer 1999.

89 ibid. We note that in the case of women, large family size might be the result of early marriage, rather than the cause of it.

90 ibid.

References

Bachrach C.A., 1980, Childlessness and social isolation among the elderly, *Journal of Marriage and the Family*, Aug 42(3), 627-636.

Berk L.M., 1977, The great middle American dream machine, *Journal of Communication*, Sum 27(3), 27-31.

Bernard, J.S., 1982, *The Future of Marriage*, Yale University Press, New Haven CT.

Blossfeld H-P, Jaenichen U., 1990, [Expanding education and its effects on the family. How does women's increasing educational level affect the postponement of marriage and children?], *Soziale Welt*, 41(4), 454-476.

Bolger N., DeLongis A., Kessler R.C., Wethington E., 1989, The contagion of stress across multiple roles, *Journal of Marriage and the Family*, Feb 51, 175-183.

Buck N., Scott J., 1993, She's leaving home: But why? An analysis of young people leaving the parental home, *Journal of Marriage and the Family*, Nov 55(4), 863-874.

Carter H., Glick P.C., 1970, *Marriage and Divorce, A Social and Economic Study*, Harvard University Press, Cambridge, MA.

Chadwick B.A., Heaton T.B., 1992, eds, *Statistical Handbook on the American Family*, Oryx Press, Phoenix.

Chalvon-Demersay S., Libbrecht L., 1995, Scenarios of crisis: Social construction of intimacy through a thousand film projects, *RESEAUX: The French Journal of Communication*, Spr 3(1), 93-110.

Coleman M., Ganong L.H., Ellis P., 1985, Family structure and dating behavior of adolescents, *Adolescence*, Fal 20(79), 537-543.

Corset P., 1995, Television viewing practices among youth: A way toward autonomy and education, *Recherches Sociologiques*, 26(1), 73-88.

Elder G.H., Rockwell R.C., 1976, Marital timing in women's life patterns, *Journal of Family History*, Fal, 1(1), 34-53.

Farquhar J., 1992, An American horror myth: Night of the Living Dead, *Semiotica*, 38(1-2), 1-15.

Gallup G.H., 1980, *The International Gallup Polls, Public Opinion, 1978*, Scholarly Resources Inc, Wilmington, DE.

Gilmartin B.G., 1985, Some family antecedents of severe shyness, *Family Relations*, 34(3), 429-438.

Goldscheider F.K., Goldscheider C., 1989, Family structure and conflict: Nest-leaving expectations of young adults and their parents, *Journal of Marriage and the Family*, Feb 51(1), 87-97.

Goldscheider F.K., LeBourdais C., 1986, The decline in age at leaving home, 1920-1979, *Sociology and Social Research*, Jan 70(2), 143-145.

Goldscheider F.K., Waite L.J., 1987, Nest leaving patterns and the transition to marriage for young men and women, *Journal of Marriage and the Family*, Aug 49(3), 507-516.

Grigsby J., McGowan J.B., 1986, Still in the nest: Adult children living with their parents, *Sociology and Social Research*, Jan 70(2), 146-148.

Gutman J., 1973, Self-concepts and television viewing among women, *Public Opinion Quarterly*, Fal 37(3), 388-397.

Hastings E.H., Hastings P.K., 1987, *Index to International Public Opinion, 1985-1986*, Greenwood Press, New York.

Herlihy D., Klapisch-Zuber C., 1985, *Tuscans and their Families*, Yale University Press, New Haven.

Hertel B.R., 1988, Gender, religious identity and work force participation, *Journal for the Scientific Study of Religion*, Dec 27(4), 574-592.

Jencks C., Crouse J., Mueser P., 1983, The Wisconsin model of status attainment: A national replication with improved measures of ability and aspirations, *Sociology of Education*, Jan 66(1), 3-19.

Kilmann P.R., Boland J.P., West M.D., Jonet C.J., et al., 1993, Sexual arousal of college students in relation to sex experiences, *Journal of Sex Education and Therapy*, Fal 19(3), 157-164.

Koller K., Gooden S., 1984, On living alone, social isolation, and psychological disorder, *The Australian and New Zealand Journal of Sociology*, Mar 20(1), 81-92.

Kuklo C., 1991, Marriage in pre-industrial Warsaw in the light of demographic studies, *Journal of Family History*, 15(3), 239-259.

Leppel K., 1987, Income effects on living arrangements: Differences between male and female householders, *Social Science Research*, Jun 16(2), 138-153.

Liehm A.J., 1975, The contemporary social film: Its content and aesthetic character, *Praxis*, Spr 1(1), 111-114.

Lipsitz G., 1990, *Time Passages: Collective Memory and American Popular Culture*, University of Minnesota Press, Minneapolis.

Malony H.N., 1988, Men and women in the clergy: Stresses, strains and resources, *Pastoral Psychology*, Spr 36(3) 164-168.

Palisi B.J., 1984, Household crowding and well-being: A cross-cultural analysis, *International Journal of Sociology of the Family*, Spr 14(1), 17-31.

Prokopec J., 1977, Determinants of interaction behavior and preference values in the choice of life partner, *Demografie*, 19(1), 11-20.

Ramu G.N., Tavuchis N, 1986, The valuation of children and parenthood among the voluntarily childless and parental couples in Canada, *Journal of Comparative Family Studies*, Spr 17(1), 99-116.

Shively J., 1991, Cultural compensation? The popularity of Westerns among American Indians, *Association Paper*.

Sporer, PD, 1999, *The Effect of Economic, Educational, Personality, and Family Factors on the Propensity to Marry*. Unpublished paper.

Sporer, P.D., 2010A, *Liberating Love*, Quenstedt Press, Chester.

Sporer, P.D., 2010B, *Equal but Different*, Quenstedt Press, Chester.

Sporer, P.D., 2010C, *The Concept of Family*, Quenstedt Press, Chester.

Stycos J.M., 1983, The timing of Spanish marriages: A socio-statistical study, *Population Studies*, Jul 37(2), 227-238.

Temple M., Polk K., 1986, A dynamic analysis of educational attainment, *Sociology of Education*, Apr 59(2), 79-84.

Teti D.M., Lamb M.E., Lester A.B., 1987, Long range socioeconomic and marital consequences of adolescent marriage in three cohorts of adult males, *Journal of Marriage and the Family*, Aug 49(3), 499-506.

Tokareva E.K., [Marriage ties and bonds of freedom], *Sotsiologicheskie Issledovaniya*, Apr 14(2), 83-91.

Trent K., 1994, Family context and adolescents' expectations about marriage, fertility, and nonmarital childbearing, *Social Science Quarterly*, Jun 75(2), 319-339.

U.S. Bureau of the Census, 1975, *Historical Statistics of the United States, Colonial Times to 1970, Bicentennial Edition, Parts 1 and 2*, Washington, DC.

U.S. Bureau of the Census, 1989, *Statistical Abstract of the United States, 1989*, (109th edition) Washington, DC.

U.S. Bureau of the Census, 1992, *Money Income of Households, Families, and Persons in the United States: 1991*, U.S. Government Printing Office, Washington, DC.

Veenhoven R., 1983, The growing impact of marriage, *Social Indicators Research*, 12(1), 49-63.

Wagner M.E., Schubert H.J., Schubert DS, 1985, Family size effects: A review, *Journal of Genetic Psychology*, Mar 146(1), 65-78.

Wenz F.V., 1984, Household crowding, loneliness and suicide ideation, *Psychology, A Quarterly Journal of Human Behavior*, 21(2), 25-29.

Willits F.K., 1988, Adolescent behavior and adult success and well-being: A 37-year panel study, *Youth and Society*, Sep 20(1), 68-87.

Wrigley E.A., 1987, *People, Cities and Wealth*, Basil Blackwell, Oxford.

Yi Z., Coale A., Choe M.K., Zhiwu L., Li L., 1994, Leaving the parental home: Census-based estimates for China, Japan, South Korea, United States, France, and Sweden, *Population Studies*, 48(1), 65-80.

Index